Physical Education and Health Study Guide

▶ ▶ ▶ ▶ ▶ ▶ ▶ ▶ ▶ ▶ ▶ ▶

A PUBLICATION OF EDUCATIONAL TESTING SERVICE

Table of Contents

Physical Education and Health Study Guide

▶   ▶   ▶   ▶   ▶   ▶   ▶   ▶   ▶   ▶   ▶   ▶

Chapter 1

Introduction to the *Physical Education* Tests and
Suggestions for Using This Study Guide   7

Chapter 2

Background Information on the Praxis Series™ Assessments   13

The *Physical Education: Content Knowledge* Test

Chapter 3

Study Topics for the *Physical Education: Content Knowledge* Test   17

Chapter 4

Don't be Defeated by Multiple-Choice Questions   25

Chapter 5

Practice Test, *Physical Education: Content Knowledge*   33

Chapter 6

Right Answers and Explanations for the Practice Test,
Physical Education: Content Knowledge   57

Physical Education: the Constructed-Response Tests

Chapter 7

Succeeding on the Physical Education Constructed-Response Tests   67

The *Physical Education: Movement Forms—Analysis and Design* Test

Chapter 8

Preparing for the *Physical Education: Movement Forms—Analysis and Design* Test   75

Chapter 9

Practice Test, *Physical Education: Movement Forms—Analysis and Design*   87

Chapter 10

Sample Responses and How They Were Scored, *Physical Education: Movement Forms—Analysis and Design* 103

The *Physical Education: Movement Forms—Video Evaluation* Test

Chapter 11

Preparing for the *Physical Education: Movement Forms—Video Evaluation* Test 129

Chapter 12

Practice Test, *Physical Education: Movement Forms—Video Evaluation* 137

Chapter 13

Sample Responses and How They Were Scored, *Physical Education: Movement Forms—Video Evaluation* 153

The *Health Education* Test

Chapter 14

Study Topics for the *Health Education* Test 165

Chapter 15

Practice Test, *Health Education* 177

Chapter 16

Right Answers and Explanations for the Practice Test, *Health Education* 195

Chapter 17

Are You Ready? 205

Appendix A

Study Plan Sheet 209

Appendix B

For More Information 211

Chapter 1

Introduction to the *Physical Education* Tests and Suggestions for Using This Study Guide

Physical Education 0091, 0092, 0093, 0550, 0856

► ► ► ► ► ► ► ► ► ► ► ►

Introduction to the *Physical Education* Tests

The *Physical Education* tests are designed for prospective secondary physical education teachers. The tests are designed to reflect current standards for knowledge, skills, and abilities in physical education. Educational Testing Service (ETS) works in collaboration with teacher educators, higher education content specialists, and accomplished practicing teachers in the field of physical education to keep the tests updated and representative of current standards.

This guide covers five different *Physical Education* tests. Some of the tests are *multiple-choice*; that is, they present questions with several possible answers choices, from which you must choose the best answer and indicate your response on an answer sheet. Other tests are *constructed-response* tests; that is, you are asked to answer a question or group of questions by writing out your response. It is not accurate to call *constructed-response* tests essay tests, since your response will not be graded on the basis of how it succeeds as an essay. Instead, your constructed response will be graded on the basis of how well it demonstrates an understanding of the principles of physical education and their appropriate application.

This guide covers the following tests:

MULTIPLE-CHOICE TESTS			
Test Name and Code	**Length of Test**	**Number and Format of Questions**	**Major Content Areas Covered and Approximate Number and Percentage of Questions in Each Area**
Physical Education: Content Knowledge (0091)	120 minutes	120 multiple-choice questions	I. Fundamental Movements, Motor Development, and Motor Learning (29 questions, 24%) II. Movement Forms (29 questions, 24%) III. Fitness and Exercise Science (23 questions, 19%) IV. Social Science Foundations (13 questions, 11%) V. Biomechanics (10 questions, 8%) VI. Health and Safety (16 questions, 14%)
Health Education (0550)	120 minutes	120 multiple-choice questions	I. Health Education as a Discipline (12 questions, 10%) II. Personal Health Care (40 questions, 33%) III. Community Health (12 questions, 10%) IV. Family Living and Sex Education (32 questions, 27%) V. Diseases and Disorders (24 questions, 20%)

| Health and Physical Education: Content Knowledge (0856) | 120 minutes | 120 multiple-choice questions | **Health**
I. Personal Health Care (19 questions, 16%)
II. Family Living and Sex Education (16 questions, 14%)
III. Community Health/Diseases and Disorders (15 questions, 12%)
Physical Education
IV. Fundamental Movements, Motor Development, and Motor Learning (22 questions, 18%)
V. Movement Forms (23 questions, 19%)
VI. Fitness and Exercise Science (25 questions, 21%) |

CONSTRUCTED-RESPONSE TESTS

Test Name and Code	Length of Test	Number and Format of Questions
Physical Education: Movement Forms—Analysis and Design (0092)	60 minutes	Two multipart constructed-response questions, each of which requires examinees to do the following: I. describe characteristics of movement forms II. design or prescribe appropriate movement routines to achieve specific goals III. provide explanatory information
Physical Education: Movement Forms—Video Evaluation (0093)	60 minutes	Two constructed-response questions, based on videotape, each of which elicits responses to visual material requiring examinees to do the following: I. describe characteristics of movement forms II. design or prescribe appropriate movement routines to achieve specific goals, detect errors, or recognize critical features in performance III. provide explanatory information

How to Use This Book

This book gives you instruction, practice, and test-taking tips to help you prepare for taking the *Physical Education* tests. In chapter 2 you will find a discussion of the Praxis Series™—what it is and how the tests are developed. If you plan to take the *Physical Education: Content Knowledge* test, you should turn to chapters 3, 4, 5, and 6 to review the topics likely to be covered on the test, get tips on succeeding at multiple-choice tests, take a practice test, and see the answers to the questions in the practice test, along with explanations of those answers. If you plan to take one or more constructed-response tests, you should turn to chapter 7 for information how to succeed on this type of test. Then chapters 8, 9, and 10 (for the *Physical Education: Movement Forms—Analysis and Design* test) and 11, 12, and 13 (for the *Physical Education: Movement Forms—Video Evaluation* test) will help you prepare for the test, take a practice test, and see sample responses and how they were scored. If you plan to take the *Health Education* test, you should turn to chapters 14, 15, and 16 to review the topics likely to be covered on the test, get tips on succeeding at multiple-choice tests, take a practice test, and see the answers to the questions in the practice test, along with explanations of those answers. Finally, if you plan to take the *Health and Physical Education: Content Knowledge* test, you should combine the materials in chapters 3, 4, 5, and 6 with the materials in chapters 14, 15, and 16.

So where should you start? Well, all users of this book will probably want to begin with the following two steps:

Become familiar with the test content. Note what the appropriate chapter of the book says about the topics covered in the test you plan to take.

Consider how well you know the content in each subject area. Perhaps you already know that you need to build up your skills in a particular area. If you're not sure, skim over the chapters that cover test content to see what topics they cover. If you encounter material that feels unfamiliar or difficult, fold down page corners or insert sticky notes to remind yourself to spend extra time in these sections.

Also, all users of this book will probably want to end with these two steps:

Familiarize yourself with test taking. Chapter 3 is designed to answer frequently asked questions about multiple-choice tests, such as whether it is a good idea to guess on a test. Similarly, chapter 7 explains how constructed-response tests are scored and contains valuable tips on how to succeed on a test in this format. With either test format, you can simulate the experience of the test by taking a practice test within the specified time limits. Choose a time and place where you will not be interrupted or distracted. After you complete the test, use the appropriate chapter(s) to score your responses to the multiple-choice questions. Look over the explanations of the questions you missed and see whether you understand them and could answer similar questions correctly. The scoring key identifies which topic each question addresses, so you can see which areas are your strongest and weakest. Then plan any additional studying according to what you've learned about your understanding of the topics and your strong and weak areas. For a constructed-response test, you can see sample responses that scored well, scored poorly, or scored in-between. By examining these sample responses, you can focus on the aspects of your own practice response that were successful and unsuccessful. This knowledge will help you plan any additional studying you might need.

Register for the test and consider last-minute tips. Consult www.ets.org/praxis/index.html to learn how to register for the test, and review the checklist in chapter 17 to make sure you are ready for the test.

What you do between these first steps and these last steps depends on whether you intend to use this book to prepare on your own or as part of a class or study group.

Using this book to prepare on your own:

If you are working by yourself to prepare for a *Physical Education* test, you may find it helpful to fill out the Study Plan Sheet in appendix A. This worksheet will help you to focus on what topics you need to study most, identify materials that will help you study, and set a schedule for doing the studying. The last item is particularly important if you know you tend to put off work.

Using this book as part of a study group:

People who have a lot of studying to do sometimes find it helpful to form a study group with others who are preparing toward the same goal. Study groups give members opportunities to ask questions and get detailed answers. In a group, some members usually have a better understanding of certain topics, while others in the group may be better at other topics. As members take turns explaining concepts to each other, everyone builds self-confidence. If the group encounters a question that none of the members can answer well, the members can go as a group to a teacher or other expert and get answers efficiently. Because study groups schedule regular meetings, group members study in a more disciplined fashion. They also gain emotional support. The group should be large enough so that various people can contribute various kinds of knowledge, but small enough so that it stays focused. Often, three to six people is a good size.

Here are some ways to use this book as part of a study group:

Plan the group's study program. Parts of the Study Plan Sheet in appendix A can help to structure your group's study program. By filling out the first five columns and sharing the work sheets, everyone will learn more about your group's mix of abilities and about the resources (such as textbooks) that members can share with the group. In the sixth column ("Dates planned for study of content"), you can create an overall schedule for your group's study program.

Plan individual group sessions. At the end of each session, the group should decide what specific topics will be covered at the next meeting and who will present each topic. Use the topic headings and subheadings in the chapter that covers the topics for the test you will take.

Prepare your presentation for the group. When it's your turn to be presenter, prepare something that's more than a lecture. Write five to ten original questions to pose to the group. Practicing writing actual questions can help you better understand the topics covered on the test as well as the types of questions you will encounter on the test. It will also give other members of the group extra practice at answering questions.

Take the practice test together. The idea of the practice test is to simulate an actual administration of the test, so scheduling a test session with the group will add to the realism and will also help boost everyone's confidence.

Learn from the results of the practice test. For each test, use the corresponding chapter with the correct answers to score each other's answer sheets. Then plan one or more study sessions based on the questions that group members got wrong. For example, each group member might be responsible for a question that he or she got wrong and could use it as a model to create an original question to pose to the group, together with an explanation of the correct answer modeled after the explanations in this study guide.

Whether you decide to study alone or with a group, remember that the best way to prepare is to have an organized plan. The plan should set goals based on specific topics and skills that you need to learn, and it should commit you to a realistic set of deadlines for meeting these goals. Then you need to discipline yourself to stick with your plan and accomplish your goals on schedule.

Chapter 2
Background Information on
the Praxis Series™ Assessments

▶ ▶ ▶ ▶ ▶ ▶ ▶ ▶ ▶ ▶ ▶ ▶

What Are The Praxis Series Subject Assessments?

The Praxis Series™ Subject Assessments are designed by Educational Testing Service (ETS) to assess your knowledge of the subject area you plan to teach, and they are a part of the licensing procedure in many states. This study guide covers an assessment that tests your knowledge of the actual content you hope to be licensed to teach. Your state has adopted The Praxis Series tests because it wants to be certain that you have achieved a specified level of mastery of your subject area before it grants you a license to teach in a classroom.

The Praxis Series tests are part of a national testing program, meaning that the test covered in this study guide is used in more than one state. The advantage of taking Praxis tests is that if you want to move to another state that uses The Praxis Series tests, you can transfer your scores to that state. Passing scores are set by states, however, so if you are planning to apply for licensure in another state, you may find that passing scores are different. You can find passing scores for all states that use The Praxis Series tests in the *Understanding Your Praxis Scores* pamphlet, available either in your college's School of Education or by calling (609) 771-7395.

What Is Licensure?

Licensure in any area—medicine, law, architecture, accounting, cosmetology—is an assurance to the public that the person holding the license has demonstrated a certain level of competence. The phrase used in licensure is that the person holding the license *will do no harm*. In the case of teacher licensing, a license tells the public that the person holding the license can be trusted to educate children competently and professionally.

Because a license makes such a serious claim about its holder, licensure tests are usually quite demanding. In some fields licensure tests have more than one part and last for more than one day. Candidates for licensure in all fields plan intensive study as part of their professional preparation: some join study groups, others study alone. But preparing to take a licensure test is, in all cases, a professional activity. Because it assesses your entire body of knowledge or skill for the field you want to enter, preparing for a licensure exam takes planning, discipline, and sustained effort. Studying thoroughly is highly recommended.

Why Does My State Require The Praxis Series Assessments?

Your state chose The Praxis Series Assessments because the tests assess the breadth and depth of content—called the "domain" of the test—that your state wants its teachers to possess before they begin to teach. The level of content knowledge, reflected in the passing score, is based on recommendations of panels of teachers and teacher educators in each subject area in each state. The state licensing agency and, in some states, the state legislature ratify the passing scores that have been recommended by panels of teachers. You can find out the passing score required for The Praxis Series Assessments in your state by looking in the pamphlet *Understanding Your Praxis Scores*, which is free from ETS (see above). If you look through this pamphlet, you will see that not all states use the same test modules, and even when they do, the passing scores can differ from state to state.

What Kinds of Tests Are The Praxis Series Subject Assessments?

Two kinds of tests comprise The Praxis Series Subject Assessments: multiple choice (for which you select your answer from a list of choices) and constructed response (for which you write a response of your own). Multiple-choice tests can survey a wider domain because they can ask more questions in a limited period of time. Constructed-response tests have far fewer questions, but the questions require you to demonstrate the depth of your knowledge in the area covered.

What Do the Tests Measure?

The Praxis Series Subject Assessments are tests of content knowledge. They measure your understanding of the subject area you want to teach. The multiple-choice tests measure a broad range of knowledge across your content area. The constructed-response tests measure your ability to explain in depth a few essential topics in your subject area. The content-specific pedagogy tests, most of which are constructed-response, measure your understanding of how to teach certain fundamental concepts in your field. The tests do not measure your actual teaching ability, however. They measure your knowledge of your subject and of how to teach it. The teachers in your field who help us design and write these tests, and the states that require these tests, do so in the belief that knowledge of subject area is the first requirement for licensing. Your teaching ability is a skill that is measured in other ways: observation, videotaped teaching, or portfolios are typically used by states to measure teaching ability. Teaching combines many complex skills, only some of which can be measured by a single test. The Praxis Series Subject Assessments are designed to measure how thoroughly you understand the material in the subject areas in which you want to be licensed to teach.

How Were These Tests Developed?

ETS began the development of The Praxis Series Subject Assessments with a survey. For each subject, teachers around the country in various teaching situations were asked to judge which knowledge and skills a beginning teacher in that subject needs to possess. Professors in schools of education who prepare teachers were asked the same questions. These responses were ranked in order of importance and sent out to hundreds of teachers for review. All of the responses to these surveys (called "job analysis surveys") were analyzed to summarize the judgments of these professionals. From their consensus, we developed the specifications for the multiple-choice and constructed-response tests. Each subject area had a committee of practicing teachers and teacher educators who wrote these specifications (guidelines). The specifications were reviewed and eventually approved by teachers. From the test specifications, groups of teachers and professional test developers created test questions.

When your state adopted The Praxis Series Subject Assessments, local panels of practicing teachers and teacher educators in each subject area met to examine the tests question by question and evaluate each question for its relevance to beginning teachers in your state. This is called a "validity study." A test is considered "valid" for a job if it measures what people must know and be able to do on that job. For the test to be adopted in your state, teachers in your state must judge that it is valid.

These teachers and teacher educators also performed a "standard-setting study"; that is, they went through the tests question by question and decided, through a rigorous process, how many questions a beginning teacher should be able to answer correctly. From this study emerged a recommended passing score. The final passing score was approved by your state's Department of Education.

In other words, throughout the development process, practitioners in the teaching field—teachers and teacher educators—have determined what the tests would contain. The practitioners in your state determined which tests would be used for licensure in your subject area and helped decide what score would be needed to achieve licensure. This is how professional licensure works in most fields: those who are already licensed oversee the licensing of new practitioners. When you pass The Praxis Series Subject Assessments, you and the practitioners in your state can be assured that you have the knowledge required to begin practicing your profession.

Chapter 3

Study Topics for the *Physical Education: Content Knowledge* Test

► ► ► ► ► ► ► ► ► ► ► ►

Introduction to the Test

The *Physical Education: Content Knowledge* test is designed to measure the professional knowledge of prospective teachers of physical education in elementary through senior high schools. The test assesses whether an examinee has the knowledge and competencies necessary for a beginning teacher of physical education.

The 120 multiple-choice questions cover knowledge of fitness, fundamental movements, and sports that comprise the content of physical education classes; knowledge of areas in the natural and social sciences that provide the foundation for teaching these activities; and knowledge of crucial topics in health and safety. Knowledge of these subject areas enables teachers to understand the nature and purpose of the activities in the physical education curriculum; to evaluate and interpret the physical characteristics and performances of students in physical education classes; and to make decisions about the ongoing conduct of physical education classes and the needs of students in those classes. Questions will test knowledge of essential facts, including the meaning of terms and placement of content elements in proper categories; understanding of relationships between and among areas of content; and the ability to apply concepts appropriately.

The content covered by the 120 questions is divided into these categories:

- Fundamental Movements, Growth and Motor Development, and Motor Learning (24%)

- Movement Forms (24%)

- Fitness and Exercise Science (19%)

- Social Science Foundations (11%)

- Biomechanics (8%)

- Health and Safety (14%)

Test takers have two hours to complete the test.

The test is not intended to assess teaching skills but rather to demonstrate the candidate's fundamental knowledge in the major areas of physical education.

Special questions marked with stars:

Interspersed throughout the list of topics are questions that are outlined in boxes and preceded by stars (★). These questions are intended to help you test your knowledge of fundamental concepts and your ability to apply the concepts to situations in the real world. Most of the questions require you to combine several pieces of knowledge in order to formulate an integrated understanding and response. If you spend time on these questions, you will gain increased understanding and facility with the subject matter covered on the test. You might want to discuss these questions and your answers with a teacher or mentor. Note that the questions marked with stars are not short-answer or multiple-choice and that this study guide does not provide the answers. The questions marked with stars are intended as study questions, not practice questions. Thinking about the answers to them should improve your understanding of fundamental concepts and will probably help you answer a broad range of questions on the test.

CONTENT DESCRIPTION

Fundamental Movements, Growth and Motor Development, and Motor Learning

Fundamental movements

- Locomotor, nonlocomotor, and manipulative

- Movement Concepts
  - ▶ Body
  - ▶ Space
  - ▶ Effort
  - ▶ Relationships
- Falling and landing movement skills

★ **How would you explain characteristics of motor skills at different stages of development?**

★ **How does motor skill development impact movement patterns?**

Growth and motor development

- Role of perception in motor development

- Effects of maturation and experience on motor patterns

- Biological and environmental influences on gender differences in motor performance

★ **What factors could influence motor development and performance?**

Motor learning

- Classical and current theories of motor learning

- Variables that affect motor learning and performance

- Effects of individual differences on motor learning and performance

★ **How would you apply various motor learning principles to skill development?**

Movement Forms

Dance and rhythmic activities

- Dance forms
  - ▶ Folk
  - ▶ Square
  - ▶ Aerobic

- Skill analysis of dance movements

★ **What rhythmic skills might be used to identify developmentally appropriate dance forms?**

★ **How would you distinguish different dance skills, and how would they be applied to different dance forms?**

Gymnastics

- Stunts and tumbling

- Use of gymnastic apparatus

- Movement themes in educational gymnastics

> ★ **In what ways might common gymnastics equipment be adapted for students of various developmental and skill levels?**

- Game Forms
    - ► Cooperative
    - ► Competitive
    - ► Invasion

- Analysis of skills, rules, and strategies of particular games

> ★ **How would you distinguish components of a game? What makes them different?**
>
> ★ **How would you explain the relationship of skills, rules, and strategies for a particular game?**

Individual/dual/team sports (emphasis on basketball, soccer, softball, swimming, tennis, track and field, and volleyball)

- Analysis of skills

- Injury prevention and safety

- Rules and strategies

- Facilities and equipment

- Activities
    - ► Lifetime
    - ► Adventure
    - ► Recreational

Fitness and Exercise Science

Components of fitness

- Cardio-respiratory

- Muscular strength and endurance

- Body composition

- Flexibility

Principles and practices of conditioning

- Frequency

- Intensity

- Time/duration

★ How could you apply the principles/practices of conditioning to fitness programs that address each of the fitness components?

★ Describe some appropriate methods for assessing fitness components.

Human biology

- Anatomy
  - ▶ Major muscles
  - ▶ Major bones
  - ▶ Body systems and their function

- Physiology
  - ▶ Terminology
  - ▶ Principles of exercise
  - ▶ Role of body systems in exercise
  - ▶ Short- and long-term effects of physical training
  - ▶ Relationship between nutrition and fitness

★ Why would understanding anatomy and physiology be important in designing and developing a physical education program?

★ How are major muscles and bones affected by various physical activities?

★ What does the current research say about fitness and exercise science?

Social Science Foundations

History of physical education

- Leading men and women, and major issues and events in the history of physical education

- Historical relationship of physical education to health and fitness

★ What were the major issues and events that helped shape the history of physical education?

Current philosophical issues

- Purpose of physical education

- Relationship between teaching and coaching

- Accountability issues as they affect physical education

- Roles, benefits, and effects of competition

★ What role has coaching played in physical education?

★ What aspects of accountability have influenced the development of physical education curriculums?

Sociological and sociopolitical issues

- Cultural diversity

- Equity
  - ▸ Title IX
  - ▸ Individuals with Disabilities Education Act (IDEA)
  - ▸ Affirmative action

- General educational issues and trends as they affect physical education

★ How has physical education been affected by issues such as state mandates, school funding, cultural diversity, Title IX, Individuals with Disabilities Education Act, and affirmative action?

Psychology

- Factors that affect student participation
  - ▸ Personality
  - ▸ Social
  - ▸ Psychological

- Cooperation among participants in various movement activities

★ Explain the effects of personality, psychological, and social influences on student participation in both cooperative and competitive environments.

Biomechanics
Terminology

- Mass

- Force

- Friction

- Levers

- Resistance

- Stability

Basic principles of movement

- Summation of forces

- Center of gravity

- Force/speed relations

- Torque

Application of Basic Principles of Movement to Sports Skills
Methods of analyzing movement

- Self-analysis

- Videotape

- Teacher and peer feedback

Analysis of basic movement patterns

- Overhand/underhand throw

- Striking skills

★ **How would you apply various biomechanical principles to the development of common skills such as punting a soccer ball?**

★ **Using biomechanics and motor learning concepts, identify stages of development for an overhand motion.**

★ **Describe some methods of analyzing movement. How can biomechanics be used in conjunction with these methods?**

Health and Safety

Safety and injury prevention

- General and specific safety considerations for all movement activities

- Safety considerations related to fitness

  ▶ Warm up/cool down

  ▶ Harmful exercise practices

  ▶ Environmental conditions

★ **How would injury prevention and safety issues be incorporated into the physical education curriculum?**

★ **Describe equipment (e.g., headgear, eyewear) that can be used to prevent injury during common physical education, sport, and recreational activities.**

Health appraisals and referrals

- Health-related fitness appraisals

- Personal goal setting and assessment

  ▶ Physical best

  ▶ President's challenge

  ▶ FITNESSGRAM®

- Considerations related to the Individuals with Disabilities Education Act

---

★ **What are the appropriate components of a fitness assessment? Why? How do they differ from those of a skill assessment?**

★ **How would fitness assessment activities be adapted for students with special needs?**

★ **How would conditioning principles shape referrals (e.g., exercise programs) intended to address the fitness needs of students?**

Handling accidents and illness

- Methods and procedures

- First aid

- Water safety

Liability and legal aspects

- Legal principles pertaining to physical education activities

  ▶ Equipment

  ▶ Class organization

  ▶ Supervision

  ▶ Program selection

★ **What kinds of liability concerns pertain to equipment, class organization, supervision, and program selection?**

★ **Describe how these concerns can be managed in physical education.**

Effects of substance abuse on performance and behavior

- Distinctions between use and abuse of substances that affect performance

- Effects of substance abuse on behavior

★ **What short- and long-term effects might a stimulant have on performance?**

★ **What behavioral changes might indicate that a student is engaging in substance abuse?**

Chapter 4

Don't Be Defeated by Multiple-Choice Questions

► ► ► ► ► ► ► ► ► ► ►

Why Multiple-Choice Tests Take Time

When you take the practice questions, you will see that there are very few simple identification questions such as "Which of the following is an example of an isometric exercise?" When The Praxis Series Assessments were first being developed by teachers and teacher educators across the country, it was almost universally agreed that prospective teachers should be able to analyze situations, synthesize material, and apply knowledge to specific examples. In short, they should be able to think as well as to recall specific facts, figures, or formulas. Consequently, you will find that you are being asked to think and to solve problems on your test. Such activity takes more time than simply answering identification questions.

In addition, questions that require you to analyze situations, synthesize material, and apply knowledge are usually longer than are simple identification questions. The Praxis Series test questions often present you with something to read (a case study, a sample of student work, a chart or graph) and ask you questions based on your reading. Strong reading skills are required, and you must read carefully. Both on this test and as a teacher, you will need to process and use what you read efficiently.

If you know your reading skills are not strong, you may want to take a reading course. College campuses have reading labs that can help you strengthen your reading skills.

Understanding Multiple-Choice Questions

You will probably notice that the word order (or syntax) in multiple-choice questions is different from the word order you're used to seeing in ordinary things you read, such as newspapers or textbooks. One of the reasons for this difference is that many such questions contain the phrase "which of the following."

The purpose of the phrase "which of the following" is to limit your choice of answers only to the list given. For example, look at this question.

Which of the following is a flavor made from beans?

(A) Strawberry
(B) Cherry
(C) Vanilla
(D) Mint

You may know that chocolate and coffee are flavors made from beans also. But they are not listed, and the question asks you to select from among the list that follows ("which of the following"). So the answer has to be the only bean-derived flavor in the list: vanilla.

Notice that the answer can be substituted for the phrase "which of the following." In the question above, you could insert "vanilla" for "which of the following" and have the sentence "Vanilla is a flavor made from beans." Sometimes it helps to cross out "which of the following" and insert the various choices. You may want to give this technique a try as you answer various multiple-choice questions in the practice test.

Also, looking carefully at the "which of the following" phrase helps you to focus on what the question is asking you to find and on the answer choices. In the simple example above, all of the answer choices are flavors. Your job is to decide which of the flavors is the one made from beans.

The vanilla bean question is pretty straightforward. But the phrase "which of the following" can also be found in more challenging questions. Look at this question:

> Which of the following practice alternatives would best promote motor learning and safety for potentially injurious sports such as pole-vaulting and downhill skiing?
>
> (A) Whole
> (B) Part
> (C) Progressive part
> (D) Distributed

The placement of "which of the following" tells you that the list of choices is a list of practice alternatives that might be used to teach sports such as these. What are you supposed to find as an answer? You are supposed to find the choice that would best promote motor learning and safety while taking into account the potential of these sports for injury.

Sometimes it helps to put the question in your own words. Here, you could paraphrase the question as "If I were teaching motor learning and safety for these sports, what kind of practice would I choose?" For a skill that has a more than average potential for injury, it is usually advisable to choose a method of practice that allows students to master specific elements of that skill under controlled conditions before that skill is attempted "whole" and under real conditions.

Choice C names a method of practice that fits this definition, and therefore it is the correct answer.

You may find that it helps to circle or underline each of the critical details of the question in your test book so that you don't miss any of them. It's only by looking at all parts of the question carefully that you will have all of the information you need to answer the question.

Circle or underline the critical parts of what is being asked in this question.

> Which of the following practice alternatives would best promote motor learning and safety for potentially injurious sports such as pole-vaulting and downhill skiing?
>
> (A) Whole
> (B) Part
> (C) Progressive part
> (D) Distributed

Here is one possible way you may have annotated the question:

> Which of the following <u>practice alternatives</u> would best promote motor learning and safety for <u>potentially injurious</u> sports such as pole-vaulting and downhill skiing?
>
> (A) Whole
> (B) Part
> (C) Progressive part
> (D) Distributed

After spending a few moments with the question, you can probably see that you are being asked to suggest a practice alternative that can build motor and safety skills in sports that have a potential for injury. Answer choices A, B, and D either do not teach all the skills required (motor learning and safety) or do not address the risks of injury. C, however, addresses all these needs for successful skill instruction and therefore is the correct answer.

The important thing is understanding what the question is asking. With enough practice, you should be able to determine what any question is asking. Knowing the answer is, of course, a different matter, but you have to understand a question before you can answer it.

Understanding questions containing "NOT," "LEAST," "EXCEPT"

In addition to "which of the following," the words "NOT," "EXCEPT," and "LEAST" often make comprehension of test questions more difficult. Because they are easily (and frequently) overlooked, these words are always capitalized when they directly impact the task presented by a test question.

For the following test question, determine what kind of answer you're looking for and what the details of the question are.

All of the following are characteristics of a correct, mature form for striking a ball with a racquet EXCEPT

(A) taking a forward step with the foot opposite to the striking arm

(B) coiling and rotating the body forward as the racquet is swung

(C) putting weight on the back foot and then shifting to the front foot as the racquet is swung

(D) stopping the racquet at the point of contact with the ball

You're looking for a characteristic that does NOT belong among those for striking a ball with a racquet when using correct, mature form. Choices A, B, and C are all generally accepted as essential elements of mature striking form. "Following through" with the swing is also an essential element, and thus D (which mentions stopping the racquet instead of following through) does NOT belong and is the correct answer.

TIP

It's easy to get confused while you're processing the information to answer a question with a LEAST, NOT, or EXCEPT in the question. If you treat the word "LEAST," "NOT," or "EXCEPT" as one of the details you must satisfy, you have a better chance of understanding what the question is asking. And when you check your answer, make "LEAST," "NOT," or "EXCEPT" one of the details you check for.

Be familiar with multiple-choice question types

Now that you have reviewed the basics of succeeding at multiple-choice questions, it should help to review the most common question formats you are likely to see.

1. Complete the statement

In this type of question, you are given an incomplete statement. You must select the choice that will make the completed statement correct.

The correct racing posture of a swimmer, a cyclist, or a downhill skier minimizes the effect of

(A) lift
(B) propulsion
(C) turbulence
(D) gravity

To check your answer, reread the question and add your answer choice at the end. Be sure that your choice best completes the sentence. The correct answer is C.

2. Which of the following

This question type is discussed in detail in a previous section. The question contains the details that must be satisfied for a correct answer, and it uses "which of the following" to limit the choices to the four choices shown, as this example demonstrates.

In the late 1800's, the greatest influence on the direction of physical education came from individuals with a background in which of the following?

(A) Medicine
(B) Professional sport
(C) Intercollegiate sport
(D) The military

The correct answer is A.

3. Roman numeral choices

This format is used when there can be more than one correct answer in the list. Consider the following example.

Angular motion is represented by which of the following?

I. The knees of a cyclist
II. The legs of a runner
III. The arms of a swimmer

(A) I only
(B) III only
(C) I and II only
(D) I, II, and III

One useful strategy in this type of question is to assess each possible answer before looking at the answer choices, then evaluate the answer choices. In the question above, you need to apply your knowledge of angular motion and of the motions performed in certain sports to identify which of the three listed options is/are examples of angular motion. You should be aware that angular motion occurs when the body or a part of it moves in a circular path about an imaginary axis called the axis of rotation. You also should know that the knees of a cyclist (option I) perform such a motion. So do the legs of a runner (option II) and the arms of the swimmer (option III). Since options I, II, and III all exemplify angular motion, the correct answer to the question is D.

4. Questions containing LEAST, EXCEPT, NOT

This question type is discussed at length above. It asks you to select the choice that doesn't fit. You must be very careful with this question type, because it's easy to forget that you're selecting the negative. This question type is used in situations in which there are several good solutions, or ways to approach something, but also a clearly wrong way.

5. Other formats

New formats are developed from time to time in order to find new ways of assessing knowledge with multiple-choice questions. If you see a format you are not familiar with, read the directions carefully. Then read and approach the question the way you would any other question, asking yourself what you are supposed to be looking for and what details are given in the question that help you find the answer.

Useful facts about the test

1. **You can answer the questions in any order.** You can go through the questions from beginning to end, as many test takers do, or you can create your own path. Perhaps you will want to answer questions in your strongest area first, and then move from your strengths to your weaker areas. There is no right or wrong way. Use the approach that works for you.

2. **There are no trick questions on the test.** You don't have to find any hidden meanings or worry about trick wording. All of the questions on the test ask about subject matter knowledge in a straightforward manner.

3. **Don't worry about answer patterns.** There is one myth that says that answers on multiple-choice tests follow patterns. There is another myth that there will never be more than two questions with the same lettered answer following each other. There is no truth to either of these myths. Select the answer you think is correct, based on your knowledge of the subject.

4. **There is no penalty for guessing.** Your test score is based on the number of correct answers you have, and incorrect answers are not counted against you. When you don't know the answer to a question, try to eliminate any obviously wrong answers and then guess at the correct one.

5. **It's OK to write in your test booklet.** You can work problems right on the pages of the booklet, make notes to yourself, mark questions you want to review later, or write anything at all. Your test booklet will be destroyed after you are finished with it, so use it in any way that is helpful to you.

Smart tips for taking the test

1. **Put your answers in the right "bubbles."** It seems obvious, but be sure that you are "bubbling in" the answer to the right question on your answer sheet. A surprising number of candidates fill in a "bubble" without checking to see that the number matches the question they are answering.

2. **Skip the questions you find to be extremely difficult.** There are bound to be some questions that you think are hard. Rather than trying to answer these on your first pass through the test, leave them blank and mark them in your test booklet so that you can come back to them. Pay attention to the time as you answer the rest of the questions on the test and try to finish with 10 or 15 minutes remaining so that you can go back over the questions you left blank. Even if you don't know the answer the second time you read the questions, see whether you can narrow down the possible answers, and then guess.

3. **Keep track of the time.** Bring a watch to the test, just in case the clock in the test room is difficult for you to see. Remember that, on average, you have one minute to answer each of the 120 questions. One minute may not seem like much time, but you will be able to answer a number of questions in only a few seconds each. You will probably have plenty of time to answer all of the questions, but if you find yourself becoming bogged down by one or more questions, you might decide to move on and come back to that section later.

4. **Read all of the possible answers before selecting one**—and then reread the question to be sure the answer you have selected really answers the question being asked. Remember that a question that contains a phrase such as "Which of the following does NOT. . ." is asking for the one answer that is NOT a correct statement or conclusion.

5. **Check your answers.** If you have extra time left over at the end of the test, look over each question and make sure that you have filled in the "bubble" on the answer sheet as you intended. Many candidates make careless mistakes that could have been corrected if they had checked their answers.

6. **Don't worry about your score when you are taking the test.** No one is expected to get all of the questions correct. Your score on this test is not analogous to your score on the SAT, the GRE, or other similar tests. It doesn't matter on this test whether you score very high or barely pass. If you meet the minimum passing scores for your state, and you meet the other requirements of the state for obtaining a teaching license, you will receive a license. Your actual score doesn't matter, as long as it is above the minimum required score. With your score report you will receive a booklet entitled *Understanding Your Praxis Scores*, which lists the passing scores for your state.

Chapter 5
Practice Test, *Physical Education: Content Knowledge*

▶   ▶   ▶   ▶   ▶   ▶   ▶   ▶   ▶   ▶   ▶   ▶

Now that you have studied the content topics and have worked through strategies related to multiple-choice questions, you should take the following practice test. You will probably find it helpful to simulate actual testing conditions, giving yourself about 90 minutes to work on the questions. You can cut out and use the answer sheet provided if you wish.

Keep in mind that the test you take at an actual administration will have different questions, although the proportion of questions in each area and major subarea will be approximately the same. You should not expect the percentage of questions you answer correctly in these practice questions to be exactly the same as when you take the test at an actual administration, since numerous factors affect a person's performance in any given testing situation.

When you have finished the practice questions, you can score your answers and read the explanations of the best answer choices in chapter 6.

Professional Assessments for Beginning Teachers®

Educational
Testing Service

TEST NAME:

Physical Education:
Content Knowledge (0091)

Time—90 Minutes

84 Multiple-Choice Questions

(Note: At the official administration of test 0091, there will be 120 multiple-choice questions, and you will be allowed 120 minutes to complete the test.)

Answer Sheet C

THE PRAXIS SERIES
Professional Assessments for Beginning Teachers®

DO NOT USE INK

Use only a pencil with soft black lead (No. 2 or HB) to complete this answer sheet.
Be sure to fill in completely the oval that corresponds to the proper letter or number.
Completely erase any errors or stray marks.

1. NAME

Enter your last name and first initial.
Omit spaces, hyphens, apostrophes, etc.

Last Name (first 6 letters) | F I

2.

YOUR NAME: (Print) _____ Last Name (Family or Surname) _____ First Name (Given) _____ M. I.

MAILING ADDRESS: (Print) _____ P.O. Box or Street Address _____ Apt. # (If any)

City _____ State or Province

Country _____ Zip or Postal Code

TELEPHONE NUMBER: ( ) _____ Home ( ) _____ Business

SIGNATURE: _____

TEST DATE: _____

3. DATE OF BIRTH

Month | Day

Jan.
Feb.
Mar.
April
May
June
July
Aug.
Sept.
Oct.
Nov.
Dec.

4. SOCIAL SECURITY NUMBER

5. CANDIDATE ID NUMBER

6. TEST CENTER / REPORTING LOCATION

Center Number _____ Room Number

Center Name _____

City _____ State or Province

Country _____

7. TEST CODE / FORM CODE

8. TEST BOOK SERIAL NUMBER

9. TEST FORM

10. TEST NAME

Educational Testing Service, ETS, the ETS logo, and THE PRAXIS SERIES:PROFESSIONAL ASSESSMENTS FOR BEGINNING TEACHERS and its logo are registered trademarks of Educational Testing Service.

ETS Educational Testing Service

51055 • 08920 • TF71M500
MH01159   Q2573-06

I.N. 202974

1   2   3   4

CERTIFICATION STATEMENT: (Please write the following statement below. DO NOT PRINT.)

"I hereby agree to the conditions set forth in the *Registration Bulletin* and certify that I am the person whose name and address appear on this answer sheet."

____

____

____

SIGNATURE: ____________________ **DATE:** ____/____/____

Month Day Year

BE SURE EACH MARK IS DARK AND COMPLETELY FILLS THE INTENDED SPACE AS ILLUSTRATED HERE: ● .

1 (A) (B) (C) (D)	**41** (A) (B) (C) (D)	**81** (A) (B) (C) (D)	**121** (A) (B) (C) (D)
2 (A) (B) (C) (D)	**42** (A) (B) (C) (D)	**82** (A) (B) (C) (D)	**122** (A) (B) (C) (D)
3 (A) (B) (C) (D)	**43** (A) (B) (C) (D)	**83** (A) (B) (C) (D)	**123** (A) (B) (C) (D)
4 (A) (B) (C) (D)	**44** (A) (B) (C) (D)	**84** (A) (B) (C) (D)	**124** (A) (B) (C) (D)
5 (A) (B) (C) (D)	**45** (A) (B) (C) (D)	**85** (A) (B) (C) (D)	**125** (A) (B) (C) (D)
6 (A) (B) (C) (D)	**46** (A) (B) (C) (D)	**86** (A) (B) (C) (D)	**126** (A) (B) (C) (D)
7 (A) (B) (C) (D)	**47** (A) (B) (C) (D)	**87** (A) (B) (C) (D)	**127** (A) (B) (C) (D)
8 (A) (B) (C) (D)	**48** (A) (B) (C) (D)	**88** (A) (B) (C) (D)	**128** (A) (B) (C) (D)
9 (A) (B) (C) (D)	**49** (A) (B) (C) (D)	**89** (A) (B) (C) (D)	**129** (A) (B) (C) (D)
10 (A) (B) (C) (D)	**50** (A) (B) (C) (D)	**90** (A) (B) (C) (D)	**130** (A) (B) (C) (D)
11 (A) (B) (C) (D)	**51** (A) (B) (C) (D)	**91** (A) (B) (C) (D)	**131** (A) (B) (C) (D)
12 (A) (B) (C) (D)	**52** (A) (B) (C) (D)	**92** (A) (B) (C) (D)	**132** (A) (B) (C) (D)
13 (A) (B) (C) (D)	**53** (A) (B) (C) (D)	**93** (A) (B) (C) (D)	**133** (A) (B) (C) (D)
14 (A) (B) (C) (D)	**54** (A) (B) (C) (D)	**94** (A) (B) (C) (D)	**134** (A) (B) (C) (D)
15 (A) (B) (C) (D)	**55** (A) (B) (C) (D)	**95** (A) (B) (C) (D)	**135** (A) (B) (C) (D)
16 (A) (B) (C) (D)	**56** (A) (B) (C) (D)	**96** (A) (B) (C) (D)	**136** (A) (B) (C) (D)
17 (A) (B) (C) (D)	**57** (A) (B) (C) (D)	**97** (A) (B) (C) (D)	**137** (A) (B) (C) (D)
18 (A) (B) (C) (D)	**58** (A) (B) (C) (D)	**98** (A) (B) (C) (D)	**138** (A) (B) (C) (D)
19 (A) (B) (C) (D)	**59** (A) (B) (C) (D)	**99** (A) (B) (C) (D)	**139** (A) (B) (C) (D)
20 (A) (B) (C) (D)	**60** (A) (B) (C) (D)	**100** (A) (B) (C) (D)	**140** (A) (B) (C) (D)
21 (A) (B) (C) (D)	**61** (A) (B) (C) (D)	**101** (A) (B) (C) (D)	**141** (A) (B) (C) (D)
22 (A) (B) (C) (D)	**62** (A) (B) (C) (D)	**102** (A) (B) (C) (D)	**142** (A) (B) (C) (D)
23 (A) (B) (C) (D)	**63** (A) (B) (C) (D)	**103** (A) (B) (C) (D)	**143** (A) (B) (C) (D)
24 (A) (B) (C) (D)	**64** (A) (B) (C) (D)	**104** (A) (B) (C) (D)	**144** (A) (B) (C) (D)
25 (A) (B) (C) (D)	**65** (A) (B) (C) (D)	**105** (A) (B) (C) (D)	**145** (A) (B) (C) (D)
26 (A) (B) (C) (D)	**66** (A) (B) (C) (D)	**106** (A) (B) (C) (D)	**146** (A) (B) (C) (D)
27 (A) (B) (C) (D)	**67** (A) (B) (C) (D)	**107** (A) (B) (C) (D)	**147** (A) (B) (C) (D)
28 (A) (B) (C) (D)	**68** (A) (B) (C) (D)	**108** (A) (B) (C) (D)	**148** (A) (B) (C) (D)
29 (A) (B) (C) (D)	**69** (A) (B) (C) (D)	**109** (A) (B) (C) (D)	**149** (A) (B) (C) (D)
30 (A) (B) (C) (D)	**70** (A) (B) (C) (D)	**110** (A) (B) (C) (D)	**150** (A) (B) (C) (D)
31 (A) (B) (C) (D)	**71** (A) (B) (C) (D)	**111** (A) (B) (C) (D)	**151** (A) (B) (C) (D)
32 (A) (B) (C) (D)	**72** (A) (B) (C) (D)	**112** (A) (B) (C) (D)	**152** (A) (B) (C) (D)
33 (A) (B) (C) (D)	**73** (A) (B) (C) (D)	**113** (A) (B) (C) (D)	**153** (A) (B) (C) (D)
34 (A) (B) (C) (D)	**74** (A) (B) (C) (D)	**114** (A) (B) (C) (D)	**154** (A) (B) (C) (D)
35 (A) (B) (C) (D)	**75** (A) (B) (C) (D)	**115** (A) (B) (C) (D)	**155** (A) (B) (C) (D)
36 (A) (B) (C) (D)	**76** (A) (B) (C) (D)	**116** (A) (B) (C) (D)	**156** (A) (B) (C) (D)
37 (A) (B) (C) (D)	**77** (A) (B) (C) (D)	**117** (A) (B) (C) (D)	**157** (A) (B) (C) (D)
38 (A) (B) (C) (D)	**78** (A) (B) (C) (D)	**118** (A) (B) (C) (D)	**158** (A) (B) (C) (D)
39 (A) (B) (C) (D)	**79** (A) (B) (C) (D)	**119** (A) (B) (C) (D)	**159** (A) (B) (C) (D)
40 (A) (B) (C) (D)	**80** (A) (B) (C) (D)	**120** (A) (B) (C) (D)	**160** (A) (B) (C) (D)

FOR ETS USE ONLY	R1	R2	R3	R4	R5	R6	R7	R8	TR	CS

PHYSICAL EDUCATION: CONTENT KNOWLEDGE

1. Which of the following activities is considered a basic locomotor skill?

   (A) Sliding
   (B) Twisting
   (C) Balancing
   (D) Throwing

2. In its most rudimentary form, which of the following locomotor skills generally appears last in a young child's repertoire of movements?

   (A) Galloping
   (B) Skipping
   (C) Hopping
   (D) Jumping

3. When young children are first learning to strike or catch a ball, they tend to focus primarily on the

   (A) flight of the ball
   (B) person throwing the ball
   (C) speed of the ball
   (D) position of their feet

4. Which of the following characteristics will be evident in the slide of a child whose sliding skills are at a mature stage of development?

   I.   The flight pattern of the body is low.
   II. Action is initiated with a step forward by the lead leg.
   III. The knees are bent during flight.
   IV. Arms and hands are held close to the body during flight.

   (A) I and III only
   (B) II and IV only
   (C) I, III, and IV only
   (D) II, III, and IV only

Questions 5–8 refer to the illustrations below.

Figure I (5-Year-Old Boy)

Figure II (6-Year-Old Girl)

Figure III (6-Year-Old Girl)

Figure IV (7-Year-Old Boy)

Figure V (9-Year-Old Girl)

5. The figures illustrate which of the following fundamental motor skills?

   (A) One-handed striking and sidearm throwing

   (B) One-handed striking and overarm throwing

   (C) Sidearm throwing and underhand throwing

   (D) Overarm throwing and underhand throwing

6. To perform the intermediate and advanced developmental levels of the skill shown in the figures safely, it is most important to limit the

   (A) length of the step

   (B) amount of the backswing

   (C) degree of trunk derotation

   (D) elbow hyperextension

7. The most rudimentary arm action of the skill shown is employed by the person in Figure

   (A) I
   (B) II
   (C) III
   (D) IV

8. The most advanced developmental level of the skill is demonstrated by the person in Figure

   (A) II
   (B) III
   (C) IV
   (D) V

9. A group of dancers are in a single circle formation with partners. The partners are facing each other with both hands joined. In this formation, which of the following movements could be performed as the first movement sequence in a children's dance?

   (A) Both partners take four walking steps forward while moving in a clockwise direction around the circle.
   (B) Both partners slide eight times to their right while moving toward the center of the circle.
   (C) Both partners gallop eight times backward while moving in a counterclockwise direction.
   (D) Both partners take four step-close movements away from the center of the circle.

10. Folk dances for grades K-2 should emphasize

    (A) tinkling steps
    (B) polka steps
    (C) locomotor skills
    (D) manipulative skills

11. The tripod (also known as the climb-up) is most commonly used as a lead-up activity for which of the following skills in stunts and tumbling?

    (A) Turk stand
    (B) Backward roll
    (C) Headstand
    (D) Wall arch

12. Which of the following is most critical to the successful performance of a headstand?

    (A) Base of support
    (B) Block rotation
    (C) Muscular strength
    (D) Muscular endurance

13. Based on the speed of the runners, which of the following is the generally accepted strategy used in setting up a pursuit relay team?

    (A) Fastest, second fastest, third fastest, slowest
    (B) Second fastest, third fastest, slowest, fastest
    (C) Third fastest, slowest, fastest, second fastest
    (D) Slowest, fastest, second fastest, third fastest

14. Developing efficient basketball skills in elementary school students can be enhanced most effectively by

(A) putting the students in a full-court, five-on-five game as soon as possible
(B) using smaller balls and lower baskets
(C) monitoring the students' knowledge of game strategies
(D) teaching passing skills before shooting skills

15. Which of the following is NOT a characteristic of mature execution of a basketball jump shot?

(A) Palm of the shooting hand in full contact with the ball
(B) Knees slightly flexed
(C) Nonshooting hand supporting the ball
(D) Shooting hand, elbow, and shoulder aligned with the target

16. Which of the following statements about the tennis volley stroke is true?

(A) It requires a long forward swing.
(B) It is used primarily from the backcourt.
(C) It is hit before the ball bounces.
(D) It is used primarily on the defensive.

17. What is the tennis score when a server has won four points and the receiver has won three points?

(A) Ad-in
(B) Ad-out
(C) 30–40
(D) 40–30

18. Using various body parts to volley a balloon or a lightweight ball will best enhance skill for which of the following sports?

(A) Basketball and soccer
(B) Basketball and tennis
(C) Volleyball and soccer
(D) Volleyball and tennis

Questions 19–20 refer to proper execution of certain volleyball skills.

19. When performing an overhand serve, the player should

(A) contact the ball with a cupped or open hand
(B) contact the ball with the arm bent
(C) serve the ball off a bounce
(D) shift weight to the back foot as the ball is contacted

20. When performing an overhead pass (set), the player should

(A) contact the ball primarily on the pads of the thumb and first two fingers
(B) keep the fingers flexible
(C) play the ball with wrist action only
(D) get into a position well behind the descending ball

21. In swimming, which of the following kicks is used in the butterfly stroke?

    (A) Dolphin
    (B) Scissor
    (C) Flutter
    (D) Whip

22. During a softball game, a base runner is hit by a batted ball while attempting to advance and before the ball passes an infielder. Which of the following rulings would be appropriate?

    (A) The ball is in play; the batter and the base runner may advance at their own risk.
    (B) The ball is in play; the base runner is out and the batter advances at his or her own risk.
    (C) The ball is dead; the base runner is awarded an extra base and the batter is out.
    (D) The ball is dead; the base runner is out and the batter is awarded first base.

23. What primary softball rule should be observed to prevent a collision between an infielder and an outfielder when a shallow fly ball is hit between them?

    (A) The fielder closer to the ball should field it.
    (B) The fielders should stay within designated zones.
    (C) The fielders should use hand signals to call the ball.
    (D) The fielders should verbally call the ball.

Questions 24–25 refer to the following list of common problems in the execution of an inside foot kick in soccer.

   I.   The kicking foot is only partially brought back prior to kicking.

  II.   The ball is contacted below its center point.

III.   The support foot is not pointed in the direction of the intended target.

IV.   The support foot is planted too far ahead of or behind the ball.

24. Which problem would most likely result in an inaccurate pass?

    (A) I
    (B) II
    (C) III
    (D) IV

25. Which problem would most likely result in the player's being off-balance?

    (A) I
    (B) II
    (C) III
    (D) IV

26. Which of the following is the most effective method of training to develop explosive leg strength in jumpers in field events?

    (A) Ballistic
    (B) Plyometric
    (C) Resistance
    (D) Speed play

27. In which two of the following events is energy production derived primarily from the aerobic energy system?

    I.   Soccer
    II. A 50-meter sprint
    III. A one-mile run
    IV. The shot put

(A)   I and II
(B)   I and III
(C)   II and III
(D)   III and IV

28. According to recent research, in a typical physical education class, most students are engaged in vigorous physical activity approximately what percentage of class time?

(A)   Less than 40%
(B)   Between 40% and 60%
(C)   Between 60% and 80%
(D)   More than 80%

29. During an exercise class, a 16-year-old student whose heart rate is 140 beats per minute would be considered to be

(A)   at ventilatory threshold
(B)   hyperventilating
(C)   performing maximal exercise
(D)   performing submaximal exercise

30. Which of the following variables best predicts the tendency to fatigue experienced by a person engaged in an aerobic activity?

(A)   The absolute rate of oxygen consumption, in liters per minute, associated with performing the activity
(B)   The weight-relative rate of oxygen consumption, in milliliters per kilogram body weight, associated with performing the activity
(C)   The percentage of individual maximal oxygen consumption (% VO_2 max) associated with performing the activity
(D)   The temperature and humidity of the environment in which the activity is performed

Questions 31–32 refer to the following workout tasks.

I. After nine circuit weight-training workouts, add three pounds to the chest-press station and ten pounds to the leg-press station.

II. Use the butterfly chest machine to help improve 100-meter breaststroke swim time.

III. Between weight-training activities, incorporate pedaling on a bicycle ergometer and rowing on a machine set to maintain a heart rate of 155 beats per minute.

IV. Run three miles carrying a five-pound weight in each hand.

31. Which task is the best example of an application of the principle of specificity?

(A) I
(B) II
(C) III
(D) IV

32. Which task is the best example of an application of the principle of progression?

(A) I
(B) II
(C) III
(D) IV

Questions 33–35 refer to the following statements.

I. The greatest amount of weight she can hold at arm's length is 2 pounds.

II. The longest he can hold a 1/4-pound weight at arm's length is 13 seconds.

III. The longest he can hold his fingertips to his toes is 2 seconds.

IV. The greatest amount of weight she can move from her side out to arm's length is 3 pounds.

33. Which statement can best be described as a measure of isometric muscular endurance?

(A) I
(B) II
(C) III
(D) IV

34. Which statement can best be described as a measure of isotonic strength?

(A) I
(B) II
(C) III
(D) IV

35. Which statement can best be described as a measure of isometric strength?

(A) I
(B) II
(C) III
(D) IV

36. Which of the following sports is generally considered to have originated in the United States and not been adapted from similar games from other countries?

    (A) Baseball
    (B) Basketball
    (C) Football
    (D) Golf

37. Physical educators in the United States who were influenced by the progressive education movement of John Dewey developed programs that emphasized

    (A) physical fitness through calisthenics
    (B) isometrics and isotonics
    (C) sports, games, and rhythm and dance
    (D) adapted activities

Questions 38–39 refer to the following Statement of Purpose of the National Association for Sport and Physical Education (NASPE) Applied Strategic Planning Team (1988).

The unique contribution that physical education and sport make is developing and maintaining attitudes, values, and practices that foster the acquisition and maintenance of physical fitness and skillful moving, joy and personal satisfaction, and the knowledge and understanding of human movement and well-being through physical activity encompassing the life span of all people.

38. The statement supports which of the following traditional categories of purposes in physical education?

    I. Organic
   II. Psychomotor
  III. Affective
  IV. Cognitive

    (A) I and II only
    (B) III and IV only
    (C) I, II, and III only
    (D) I, II, III, and IV

39. The statement most nearly reflects which of the following statements about human nature?

    (A) Human beings have minds and bodies that are distinct from one another and act on one another (interactionism).
    (B) Human beings have minds that control and direct their bodies (dualistic idealism).
    (C) Human beings are an integration of physical and mental aspects (holism).
    (D) Human beings have separate but equal mental and physical lives (parallelism).

40. Which of the following lists the usual developmental order of play stages through which children progress in United States society?

    (A)   Competitive, cooperative, introspective, parallel

    (B)   Cooperative, competitive, parallel, introspective

    (C)   Introspective, parallel, cooperative, competitive

    (D)   Parallel, cooperative, competitive, introspective

41. Which of the following best describes the effect of sports participation on personality?

    (A)   Players are not affected in a predictable way.

    (B)   Players who pursue individual sports become more introverted.

    (C)   Players who participate in team sports become more extroverted.

    (D)   Players tend to become more individualistic.

42. A "primary group," as the term is used by social scientists, is best characterized as which of the following?

    (A)   Competitive and large in number, with intermittent contact between members

    (B)   Small and intimate, with face-to-face contact between members

    (C)   Impersonal, informal, and contractual

    (D)   Impersonal, contractual, and cooperative

Questions 43–44 refer to research findings on child development and game playing.

43. Which of the following statements best characterizes most children between the ages of 5 and 8 ?

    (A)   They are in the egocentric stage.

    (B)   They choose leaders spontaneously from among themselves.

    (C)   They are primarily concerned with following the rules.

    (D)   They begin to create strategies and mentally test their abilities.

44. Which of the following statements best characterizes most children between the ages of 8 and 11 ?

    (A)   They have lost their strong egocentric tendencies.

    (B)   They have a strong social need, especially at the higher age range.

    (C)   They have a desire to participate in parallel play.

    (D)   They feel more comfortable as part of a large group than as part of a small group.

45. On a continuum from closed skills to open skills, which of the following best represents the correct placement of driving from the tee in golf and hitting ground strokes in tennis?

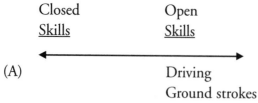

	Closed Skills	Open Skills
(A)		Driving Ground strokes
(B)	Driving Ground strokes	
(C)	Driving	Ground strokes
(D)	Ground strokes	Driving

46. When a basketball player takes a shot and completely misses the rim, the net, and the backboard, the crowd's chant of "Airball" can be best described as an example of which of the following types of feedback?

    (A) Intrinsic knowledge of results
    (B) Extrinsic knowledge of results
    (C) Intrinsic knowledge of performance
    (D) Extrinsic knowledge of performance

47. Which of the following terms describes a type of feedback that is exclusively intrinsic?

    (A) Knowledge of results
    (B) Knowledge of performance
    (C) Videotape replays
    (D) Proprioception

48. A skilled free-throw basketball shooter who misses a free throw by hitting the front rim has most likely committed an error in which of the following phases of information processing?

    (A) Input
    (B) Decision making
    (C) Output
    (D) Feedback

49. Which of the following statements best describes the relationship of mental practice to performance?

    (A) Mental practice can replace physical practice.
    (B) Mental practice works best with skilled individuals and familiar tasks. [x]
    (C) Mental practice should never be used for pre-performance rehearsal.
    (D) Mental practice works best when the skill is thought about without reference to its performance context.

50. For high school-aged and adult learners, the three phases of motor learning typically occur in which of the following sequences?

    (A) Cognitive, associative, autonomous
    (B) Cognitive, autonomous, associative
    (C) Autonomous, cognitive, associative
    (D) Associative, cognitive, autonomous

51. A group of children share the following characteristics:

- They run with control over their starting, stopping, and turning.
- Slightly fewer than half attempt to gallop.
- About one-third are proficient at hopping.
- On a one-foot-wide beam, about two-thirds can touch a knee down and regain a standing position.
- They can do a standing long jump of eight to ten inches.

The children would most likely first share these characteristics at the age of

(A) 2 years
(B) 4 years
(C) 6 years
(D) 8 years

52. A group of children share the following characteristics:

- They are able to use a knife for cutting and spreading.
- They can draw horizontal and vertical lines but still have difficulty with oblique lines.
- They can copy a square and a triangle but not a diamond.
- They can color within lines and cut fairly accurately.

The children would most likely first share these characteristics at the age of

(A) 1 year
(B) 3 years
(C) 5 years
(D) 7 years

53. Which of the following statements about the running pattern is LEAST accurate?

(A) The foot lands directly under the center of gravity in the mature pattern.
(B) The length of the bilateral arm swing is greater in the mature pattern than in the immature pattern.
(C) The base of support is wider in the immature pattern than in the mature pattern.
(D) There is less hip flexion of the striding leg in the mature pattern than in the immature pattern.

54. In children aged 5 through 9, the largest gender difference is generally evident in which of the following?

(A) Standing height (or stature)
(B) Overarm throwing velocity and distance
(C) Standing long jump distance
(D) Sprint running speed and duration

55. When a child is learning to catch a ball, the avoidance reaction can be minimized by having the child practice catching a

(A) baseball
(B) tennis ball
(C) yarn ball
(D) volleyball

56. Which of the following statements about the mature overhand throwing pattern is true?

    (A) The forearm lags behind the upper arm and shoulder during the forward movement.
    (B) The throwing action begins with a push-off on the forward leg.
    (C) The forearm and the upper arm move forward as one segment.
    (D) The nonthrowing hand remains close to the body until release.

57. All of the following statements about children's growth and development are true EXCEPT:

    (A) Evaluating the specific components of weight, fat, and lean body tissue provides better information about children's development than evaluating their height and weight.
    (B) The changing of body proportions caused by growth and development (e.g., shoulder-hip ratio, standing-sitting height ratio) frequently influences children's motor performances.
    (C) Differences in the postpubescent performances of boys and girls are only partly due to boys' increased size and strength.
    (D) Biological maturity can be estimated by skeletal age; however, chronological age is a better way to estimate the degree of maturity.

58. An instructor could best assist a young, inexperienced roller to advance to the next developmental level of the forward roll by

    (A) showing films of gymnastic events with gymnasts doing aerial somersaults
    (B) describing in great detail how the child should perform an advanced-level forward roll
    (C) providing a variety of readiness experiences, especially ones that involve weight bearing on the hands and curling the body
    (D) praising the child for all attempts at rolling regardless of performance

59. Performance of which of the following can be classified as an aerobic activity?

    I.   A 10-kilometer (6-mile) cross-country run
    II. A golf swing
    III. A soccer game
    IV. A high jump
    V.   A football play

    (A) I only
    (B) I and III only
    (C) II and IV only
    (D) I, IV, and V only

60. Positive mood shifts often accompany sustained exercise. Current research indicates that this can most likely be attributed to which of the following?

    (A) Biochemical changes only
    (B) Developmental changes only
    (C) Psychological changes only
    (D) Both biochemical and psychological changes

61. Which of the following activities would most likely result in the highest level of blood lactate accumulation?

   (A)   A 50-yard dash
   (B)   A 400-yard dash
   (C)   A 3-mile walk at a brisk pace
   (D)   A 30-minute jog at a comfortable pace

62. As a measure of physical fitness, the maximal oxygen consumption of an individual reflects the adaptation of all of the following aspects of bodily functioning EXCEPT

   (A)   lung ventilation
   (B)   pulmonary diffusion
   (C)   maximum heart rate
   (D)   cardiac function

63. After maturity, which of the following generally increases due to the aging process?

   (A)   Maximum heart rate
   (B)   Vital capacity
   (C)   Body fat
   (D)   Body height

64. After maturity, which of the following generally decreases due to the aging process?

   (A)   Aerobic capacity
   (B)   Resting systolic blood pressure
   (C)   Resting heart rate
   (D)   Residual volume

65. A high school student running the 400-meter dash uses which of the following major energy systems?

   (A)   The ATP-PC (phosphocreatine) system only
   (B)   The lactic acid system only
   (C)   The oxygen system only
   (D)   Both the ATP-PC and lactic acid systems

66. The line of the pulling force of a muscle at a joint may be considered a vector that can be resolved into which of the following pairs of components?

   (A)   Anatomical and physiological
   (B)   Direct and indirect
   (C)   Vertical and horizontal
   (D)   Actual and theoretical

67. If the effect of a load placed at the end of an extremity, such as a weight in the hand, is greater than the effect produced by the musculature contracting in opposition to the load, the resulting muscular contraction will be

   (A)   eccentric
   (B)   isokinetic
   (C)   isometric
   (D)   concentric

Questions 68–69 refer to the following series of sketches, which depict the beginning, middle, and final phases in the performance of one repetition of the illustrated exercise.

POSITION I

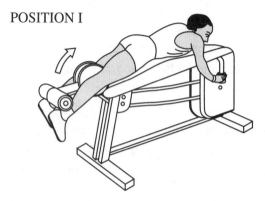

POSITION II

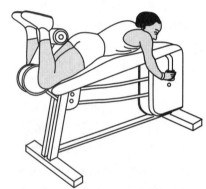

Pause for 2-4 seconds in this position.

POSITION III

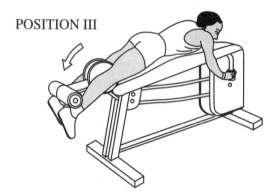

68. This exercise can be most effectively used to strengthen which of the following muscles?

(A) Hip adductor
(B) Quadriceps
(C) Anterior deltoid
(D) Hamstring

69. As the exercise is performed from positions I through III, with a pause of 2 to 4 seconds at position II, the sequence of muscle contractions that occurs is best described by which of the following?

(A) Concentric, eccentric, isometric
(B) Concentric, isometric, eccentric
(C) Eccentric, concentric, isometric
(D) Eccentric, isometric, concentric

70. The "clean and jerk" motion in weight lifting, an aggressive rebound in basketball, and a sprinter's start are all considered power moves, because these skills effectively combine which of the following factors?

    (A) Torque and distance
    (B) Time and distance
    (C) Work and distance
    (D) Work and time

71. Which of the following principles of stability is best exemplified when a gymnast squats to regain balance on the balance beam?

    (A) The line of gravity intersecting the base of support affords better stability.
    (B) A longer base of support affords better stability.
    (C) A wider base of support affords better stability.
    (D) A lower center of gravity affords better stability.

72. The human body's center of gravity is a point that

    (A) is generally in the same position for males and females
    (B) remains unchanged regardless of any movement of body parts
    (C) can be within or outside the body, depending on body posture
    (D) varies with body position but remains located within the body

73. Heavy resistive training, such as strenuous weight training, should be avoided in early childhood because of the potential development of

    (A) inflexible joints
    (B) epiphyseal separations
    (C) elongated ligaments
    (D) calcium deposits

74. Following vigorous aerobic exercise, a proper cooling-down period should involve which of the following activities?

    I.   Walking
    II. Stretching
    III. Rope jumping

    (A) I only
    (B) I and II only
    (C) II and III only
    (D) I, II, and III

75. Which of the following is the most appropriate safety measure a teacher can use for an asthmatic individual who will be participating in a volleyball game?

    (A) Limiting duration of participation
    (B) Adapting equipment or facilities
    (C) Modifying the rules
    (D) Adapting the skills

76. Which of the following sequences would be most appropriate for the first 10 minutes of an exercise session that includes playing 30 minutes of nonstop soccer?

   (A)   Stretching, jogging, wind sprints, calisthenics
   (B)   Stretching, calisthenics, jogging, wind sprints
   (C)   Jogging, calisthenics, stretching, wind sprints
   (D)   Jogging, wind sprints, calisthenics, stretching

77. Which of the following physical fitness components would most likely be assessed in a battery of health-related physical fitness tests?

   (A)   Agility
   (B)   Power
   (C)   Muscle strength
   (D)   Dynamic balance

78. To lose one pound of fat per week, a person would theoretically need a weekly caloric deficit of approximately

   (A)   1,500 calories
   (B)   3,500 calories
   (C)   5,500 calories
   (D)   7,500 calories

79. Which of the following would have the most direct effect of minimizing the risk of heart disease?

   (A)   Avoiding alcoholic beverages
   (B)   Avoiding smoking
   (C)   Having an annual physical examination
   (D)   Having hormone therapy

80. A student suffers an injury while running. The teacher questions the student about how the injury occurred and about the area of the body affected and examines the area indicated. The symptoms are typical of a sprained ankle, although the injury may in fact be more severe. Which of the following steps should be included in the first aid administered immediately to this student?

   I.   Elevate the injured part.
   II.   Apply ice to the injured area.
   III. Apply direct pressure to the site of the injury.

   (A)   I only
   (B)   II only
   (C)   I and II only
   (D)   I and III only

81. Which of the following best explains why drownproofing (survival float) is superior to treading water as a swimming survival skill?

   (A)   Drownproofing is based on the "buddy system," so a second person is available to help.
   (B)   Drownproofing permits the use of a wider variety of leg and arm movements.
   (C)   Treading water requires the use of emergency equipment, and this equipment may not be available.
   (D)   Treading water uses more effort, so it cannot be sustained for as long a period.

82. A signed consent form should be obtained from the parent or guardian of a student who is going on a sport or adventure field trip because the form

    (A) signifies that the parent or guardian assumes primary responsibility for anything that might happen on the trip

    (B) shows the teacher that the parent or guardian knows what activity is planned for the student and does not object

    (C) prevents a parent or guardian from successfully suing the teacher if a student is injured

    (D) relieves the school district of responsibility for the student

83. What kind of drug is crack?

    (A) A depressant
    (B) A narcotic
    (C) A stimulant
    (D) A hallucinogen

84. Which of the following drugs is generally considered a depressant?

    (A) Cocaine
    (B) LSD
    (C) Alcohol
    (D) Marijuana

Chapter 6

Right Answers and Explanations for the Practice Test,
Physical Education: Content Knowledge

▶   ▶   ▶   ▶   ▶   ▶   ▶   ▶   ▶   ▶   ▶   ▶

Now that you have answered all of the practice questions, you can check your work. Compare your answers with the correct answers in the table below.

Question Number	Correct Answer	Content Category	Question Number	Correct Answer	Content Category
1	A	Fundamental movements	43	A	Psychology
2	B	Fundamental movements	44	B	Psychology
3	B	Fundamental movements	45	C	Motor learning
4	A	Fundamental movements	46	B	Motor learning
5	D	Fundamental movements	47	D	Motor learning
6	D	Fundamental movements	48	C	Motor learning
7	C	Fundamental movements	49	B	Motor learning
8	C	Fundamental movements	50	A	Motor learning
9	D	Movement forms	51	B	Growth and motor development
10	C	Movement forms	52	C	Growth and motor development
11	C	Movement forms	53	D	Growth and motor development
12	A	Movement forms	54	B	Growth and motor development
13	B	Movement forms	55	C	Growth and motor development
14	B	Movement forms	56	A	Growth and motor development
15	A	Movement forms	57	D	Growth and motor development
16	C	Movement forms	58	C	Growth and motor development
17	A	Movement forms	59	B	Human biology
18	C	Movement forms	60	D	Human biology
19	A	Movement forms	61	B	Human biology
20	A	Movement forms	62	C	Human biology
21	A	Movement forms	63	C	Human biology
22	D	Movement forms	64	A	Human biology
23	D	Movement forms	65	D	Human biology
24	C	Movement forms	66	C	Biomechanics
25	D	Movement forms	67	B	Biomechanics
26	B	Movement forms	68	D	Human biology
27	B	Fitness	69	B	Biomechanics
28	A	Fitness	70	D	Biomechanics
29	D	Fitness	71	D	Biomechanics
30	C	Fitness	72	C	Biomechanics
31	B	Fitness	73	B	Injury prevention & safety
32	A	Fitness	74	B	Injury prevention & safety
33	B	Fitness	75	A	Injury prevention & safety
34	D	Fitness	76	C	Injury prevention & safety
35	A	Fitness	77	C	Health appraisals and referrals
36	B	History	78	B	Health appraisals and referrals
37	C	History	79	B	Health appraisals and referrals
38	D	Current issues	80	C	Handling accidents & illnesses
39	C	Current issues	81	D	Water safety & certification
40	C	Sociological/sociopolitical issues	82	B	Liability/legal aspects
41	A	Sociological/sociopolitical issues	83	C	Effects of Substance Abuse
42	B	Psychology	84	C	Effects of Substance Abuse

Explanations of Right Answers

1. Sliding involves moving sideways. It is, therefore, considered a basic locomotor skill (i.e., it is characterized by moving from one location to another). The correct answer, therefore, is A.

2. Skipping is a combination of a step and a hop. Combining these skills is characteristically difficult for children at earlier stages of development. The correct answer, therefore, is B.

3. Young children are characteristically distracted by the motion of the person throwing the ball. The correct answer, therefore, is B.

4. At the mature stage, the student maintains a low center of gravity, maintains flexion in the knees, and steps sideways to begin the movement pattern. The correct answer, therefore, is A.

5. The arm of the student clearly shows in Figure I an underhand throwing motion. In the other illustrations, the arm is moving over the shoulder—performing an overhand throw. The correct answer, therefore, is D.

6. "Tennis" or "little league" elbow results from hyperextension of the elbow. It is often associated with throwing by prepubescent individuals and the use of such skills as "curve ball" throwing. The correct answer, therefore, is D.

7. In Figure III there is very little movement of the body. The throw is executed with the arm only. The correct answer, therefore, is C.

8. Figure IV shows utilization of many of the proper mechanics of a throw: a proper starting point with the arm, and the proper rotation of the elbow through the release of the ball. The body is properly positioned to start the throwing sequence. It shows rotation and transfer of weight. The correct answer, therefore, is C.

9. In choice D the dancers create space by moving away from the middle of the circle. This allows the circle to become bigger, allowing different types of movement activity. The movements in choices A, B, and C would cause the dancers to run into each other, or cause one partner to move in a manner contrary to the description provided. The correct answer, therefore, is D.

10. For students in grades K-2, dance activities should emphasize the development of locomotor skills. The correct answer, therefore, is C.

11. This activity establishes the proper base of support for the headstand. It also allows elements of the headstand to be taught in a sequence of movements. The correct answer, therefore, is C.

12. Performing a headstand requires little in the way of muscular strength (choice C) or endurance (choice D). Although these components can be helpful when holding the headstand for an extended period, neither can compensate for an inadequate base of support, choice A. Block rotation (choice B) is not used at all when performing a headstand. The correct answer, therefore, is A.

13. The common strategy is to get off to a fast start and finish with the fastest runner. The correct answer, therefore, is B.

14. Children's hands are smaller, and many times they lack the strength to reach a regulation-height basket. Smaller balls and lower baskets allow the children a better chance to succeed. The correct answer, therefore, is B.

15. The ball should be positioned on the finger pads when a basketball jump shot is being made. The correct answer, therefore, is A.

16. The volley is used to return the ball quickly over the net. This means that the ball is struck before it hits the ground. The correct answer, therefore, is C.

17. The server's score is the second score given. After 4 points (at game point), the following terms are used in conjunction with Ad: In (server's advantage), Ad: Out (receiver's advantage), or Deuce (even score). The correct answer, therefore, is A.

18. In both volleyball and soccer, one of the tasks is to volley the ball with various body parts. The correct answer, therefore, is C.

19. When executing an overhand serve, a volleyball player contacts the ball with the heel of a cupped or open hand to provide for surface coverage of the ball and to exert control over the ball. The correct answer, therefore, is A.

20. Using the finger pads allows a player to direct the set pass and release it quickly. The correct answer, therefore, is A.

21. The butterfly stroke utilizes the dolphin kick. The correct answer, therefore, is A.

22. The situation described is known as a dead-ball foul. The rule described in choice D applies (as it also does in baseball), making that the correct answer.

23. When fielding a fly ball, the players are to listen for verbal calls from each other. This type of communication will eliminate most collisions. The correct answer, therefore, is D.

24. The support foot aligns the hips to the direction of the kick. Having the support foot not pointed at the target causes the hips to misdirect the ball. The correct answer, therefore, is C.

25. The support foot should be planted alongside the ball. If the support foot is planted too far ahead of or behind the ball, the player will not have proper balance on either foot. The correct answer, therefore, is D.

26. Plyometric training addresses, from the standpoint of specificity, explosive movements (rapid isotonic contractions). The correct answer, therefore, is B. Note: Care should be taken when using plyometric training. Its use with young athletes may carry a risk of injury.

27. Soccer and the one-mile run involve longer periods of cardiorespiratory exertion. The correct answer, therefore, is B.

28. Research on classes that ranged in time between 30 and 40 minutes found less than 40% of the time being spent on vigorous physical activity. The correct answer, therefore, is A.

29. For a physically normal student of age 16, the THR zone for maximal exercise is well above 140 BPM. The correct answer, therefore, is D.

30. Fatigue is predicted by the percentage of oxygen consumed in relation to the intensity of the activity. The correct answer, therefore, is C.

31. The butterfly chest machine isolates the muscles of the upper body, and use of the machine closely simulates the action of the breast stroke. The correct answer, therefore, is B.

32. A gradual increase in weight allows the muscles to train at one weight and progress to the next when ready. The correct answer, therefore, is A.

33. The second statement describes maintaining a static muscle position over time, which is the definition of isometric muscular endurance. The correct answer, therefore, is B.

34. The last statement describes moving the muscle through a range of motion against a resistance, which is the definition of isotonic strength. The correct answer, therefore, is D.

35. The first statement describes maintaining a static muscle position against a resistance, which is the definition of isometric strength. The correct answer, therefore, is A.

36. Basketball was developed at a YMCA in Massachusetts as an indoor exercise activity for men who did not want to play football outside during the winter. The correct answer, therefore, is B.

37. Sports, games, and rhythm and dance were taught in the early physical education programs. These still form the foundation of current physical education curriculums. The correct answer, therefore, is C.

38. The terms "organic," "psychomotor," "affective," and "cognitive" are the core domains of physical education. The statement addresses each of these domains. The correct answer, therefore, is D.

39. The philosophy of mind-body integrity lies at the foundation of modern physical education practice. Choice C addresses the needs of both mind and body together and, therefore, is the correct answer.

40. The sequence "introspective, parallel, cooperative, competitive" places the phases in their correct order. The correct answer, therefore, is C.

41. Sports participation will impact players in a variety of different ways. Research does not support the common notion that sport participation affects or develops participants' personalities in any predictable way. The correct answer, therefore, is A.

42. The defining characteristics of a primary group are that it is small and intimate, with face-to-face contact between members. The correct answer, therefore, is B.

43. Children at this age are concerned with their own needs. Their environment is primarily centered on the self. The correct answer, therefore, is A.

44. Children become increasingly aware of their environment and the individuals who influence their surroundings. There is a greater need to interact with people and other stimuli in these settings. The correct answer, therefore, is B.

45. Closed skills refer to actions initiated by the performer on stationary objects (e.g., driving). In open skills (e.g., tennis ground strokes), the objects are already moving. The correct answer, therefore, is C.

46. The crowd responds to the outcome (result) of the player's performance. The correct answer, therefore, is B.

47. Proprioception refers to a feeling within—the physical feeling the performer has regarding the completed task. The correct answer, therefore, is D.

48. Output refers to outcome in relation to the intended goal. The correct answer, therefore, is C.

49. In order for mental practice to work, an individual must know the task and have the skills to perform the task. The correct answer, therefore, is B.

50. Learners of high school or adult age need to follow this sequence: understand the skill, connect it to other skills or previous learning, and then perform the task almost automatically. (The last stage gives the performer opportunities to attend less to skill performance and more to other aspects of the task, such as ball placement or strategy.) The correct answer, therefore, is A.

51. Generally, at age 4 students have acquired some degree of locomotor skill, a developed sense of balance, and strength with one foot. The correct answer, therefore, is B.

52. Generally, fine motor skills are refined enough at age 5 to accomplish these tasks. The correct answer, therefore, is C.

53. Hip flexion is increased in the striding leg in a mature running pattern. The correct answer, therefore, is D.

54. At these ages the most profound gender differences are in positioning of the arm and trunk, plus leg mechanics. The correct answer, therefore, is B. The physical education professional needs to be concerned with providing sufficient practice opportunities for female students in order to help address these differences.

55. A yarn ball is soft and will not hurt the child. It is easier to absorb the force of this ball, so the child is less likely to be afraid of it. The correct answer, therefore, is C.

56. In the mature sequence, the shoulder and upper arm lead, then the forearm, wrist, and ball follow when one is throwing overhand. The correct answer, therefore, is A.

57. Skeletal age is a better indication of maturity than chronological age. The correct answer, therefore, is D.

58. The activities described in choice C provide the best progression toward promoting rolling development. Forward rolling requires a number of skills, such as taking weight on the arms, getting into an inverted position, and maintaining a "curl." The correct answer, therefore, is C.

59. In a 10-kilometer cross-country run and a soccer game, performances require long periods of running without rest, involving cardiorespiratory endurance. The correct answer, therefore, is B.

60. In addition to a stronger sense of self-esteem, exercise causes chemical releases that enhance positive mood shifts. The correct answer, therefore, is D.

61. During the 400-yard dash, the extreme intensity of the physical activity overtakes the circulatory system's ability to remove blood lactate from the muscles. The correct answer, therefore, is B.

62. Maximum heart rate does not directly reflect oxygen consumption. The correct answer, therefore, is C.

63. With age, ever-greater percentages of body cells become less metabolically active, generally causing more body fat to accumulate over time. The correct answer, therefore, is C.

64. Pulmonary diffusion generally decreases with age, directly impacting the overall capacity of the body's aerobic system. The correct answer, therefore, is A.

65. Both the ATP-PC and lactic acid systems are used in running the 400-meter dash. The muscles use ATP-PC and fatigue due to the buildup of lactic acid. The correct answer, therefore, is D.

66. Only choice C lists components of vector resolution. The correct answer, therefore, is C.

67. The isokinetic sequence represents pulling the weight (shortening the muscles), holding the weight, and finally lengthening the muscles while still resisting the weight. The correct answer, therefore, is B.

68. Raising the weight with the legs on this apparatus is usually referred to as doing hamstring curls. The correct answer, therefore, is D.

69. Position I illustrates a concentric muscle contraction, which is defined as a shortening contraction during which the overall length of the muscle becomes shorter. The pause at position II illustrates an isometric contraction, i.e., one in which no change in muscle length takes place. Position III illustrates an eccentric contraction, i.e., a lengthening, in a controlled manner, of a previously tensed muscle. The correct answer, therefore, is B.

70. These tasks are explosive movements and thus must be executed in a short period of time with great force. The correct answer, therefore, is D.

71. The lower the gymnast is to the balance beam, the more stable the distribution of weight over the base. The correct answer, therefore, is D.

72. The idea that the human body's center of gravity can be within or outside the body, depending on body posture, is a basic biomechanical principle. The correct answer, therefore, is C.

73. For young children, such training could damage the growth plates or growth areas in the bone, typically through epiphyseal separations. The correct answer, therefore, is B.

74. Stretching helps reduce lactic acid build-up (which can contribute to muscle soreness). Walking brings the heart rate down gradually to its resting pulse rate. The correct answer, therefore, is B.

75. For a condition that impacts the aerobic capacity of an individual student, modifying the duration of that student's activity allows that student the benefits of participation without impacting the nature of the activity for the rest of the participants. The correct answer, therefore, is A.

76. Jogging will increase the blood flow to the muscles, thus enhancing the effectiveness of the callisthenic and stretching exercises. This sequence minimizes the likelihood of injury to muscles by placing activities in an appropriate warm-up sequence. The correct answer, therefore, is C.

77. The components listed in choices A, B, and D would be found in a skill-related (rather than health-related) test battery. The correct answer, therefore, is C.

78. 3,500 calories = 1 pound: This deficit should be reflected through food intake. The correct answer, therefore, is B.

79. Smoke from cigarettes clogs and closes arteries and lung passages. This causes extra strain on the heart. The correct answer, therefore, is B.

80. Ice and elevation will help to control swelling. Direct pressure may cause more serious injury. The correct answer, therefore, is C. Any treatment that may result in pressure on the injured area (such as an Ace bandage applied to the whole ankle) should be carried out by an athletic trainer or other qualified professional.

81. Treading water expends significantly more energy than does drownproofing (survival float). The correct answer, therefore, is D.

82. Consent forms are primarily informational documents. The teacher is still primarily responsible for the student's safety during the trip. The correct answer, therefore, is B.

83. Chemical stimulants generally increase the rate of most body functions, which is the effect that crack cocaine has. The correct answer, therefore, is C.

84. Chemical depressants generally decrease the rate of most body functions, which is the effect that alcohol has. (Note: Marijuana is not classified as a depressant.) The correct answer, therefore, is C.

Chapter 7

Succeeding on the Physical Education Constructed-Response Tests

▶   ▶   ▶   ▶   ▶   ▶   ▶   ▶   ▶   ▶   ▶   ▶

The goal of this chapter is to provide you with background information, advice from experts, and close examination of sample questions and responses so that you can improve your skills in writing answers to constructed-response questions related to human movement. This chapter focuses on producing your response—making sure you understand what the question is asking and then using advice from experts to formulate a successful response.

What You Should Know About How the Physical Education Constructed-Response Tests Are Scored

As you build your skills in writing answers to constructed-response questions, it is important to have in mind the process used to score the tests. If you understand where your test goes and how experts determine your scores, you may have a better context in which to think about your strategies for success.

How the Tests Are Scored

After each test administration, test books are returned to ETS. The test booklets in which constructed-response answers are written are sent to the location of the "scoring session."

The scoring sessions usually take place over two days. The sessions are led by "scoring leaders," highly qualified physical education teachers who have many years' experience scoring test questions. All of the remaining scorers are experienced physical education teachers and physical education teacher-educators. An effort is made to balance experienced scorers with newer scorers at each session; the experienced scorers provide continuity with past sessions, and the new scorers ensure that new ideas and perspectives are considered, and that the pool of scorers remains large enough to cover the test's needs throughout the year.

Preparing to train the scorers

The scoring leaders meet several days before the scoring session to assemble the materials for the training portions of the main session. Training scorers is a rigorous process, and it is designed to ensure that each response gets a score that is consistent both with the scores given to other papers and with the overall scoring philosophy and criteria established for the test when it was first designed.

The scoring leaders first review the General Scoring Guides, which contain the overall criteria, stated in general terms, for awarding the appropriate score. The leaders also review and discuss—and make additions to, if necessary—the Question-Specific Scoring Guides, which serve as applications of the general guide to each specific question on the test. The question-specific guides cannot cover every possible response the scorers will see, but they are designed to give enough examples to guide the scorers in making accurate judgments about the variety of answers they will encounter.

To begin identifying appropriate training materials for an individual question, the scoring leaders first read through many responses to get a sense of the range of answers. They then choose a set of benchmarks, one paper at each score level. These benchmarks serve as solid representative examples at each score level and are considered the foundation for score standards throughout the session.

The scoring leaders then choose a larger set of test-taker responses to serve as sample papers. These sample papers represent a wide variety of possible responses that the scorers might see. The sample papers serve as the basis for practice scoring at the scoring session, so that the scorers can rehearse how they will apply the scoring criteria before they begin.

The process of choosing a set of benchmark responses and a set of sample responses is followed systematically for each question to be scored at the session. After the scoring leaders are done with their selections and discussions, the sets they have chosen are photocopied and inserted into the scorers' folders in preparation for the session.

Training at the main scoring session

At the scoring session, the scorers are placed into groups according to the question they are assigned to score. New scorers are distributed equally across all questions. One of the scoring leaders is placed with each group. The Chief Scorer is the person who has overall authority over the scoring session and plays a variety of key roles in training and in ensuring consistent and fair scores.

For each question, the training session proceeds the same way:

1. All scorers carefully read through the question they will be scoring.

2. All scorers review the "General Scoring Guide" and the "Question-Specific Scoring Guide" for the question.

3. For each question, the leader guides the scorers through the set of benchmark responses, explaining in detail why each response received the score it did. Scorers are encouraged to ask questions and share their perspectives.

4. Scorers practice on the set of samples chosen by the leaders. The leader polls the scorers on what scores they awarded and then leads a discussion to ensure that there is a consensus about the scoring criteria and how they are to be applied.

5. One or more sets of nonscored papers are then read by each member of the group. A discussion of scores awarded and the scoring criteria follows each reading set. The papers are then scored using a consensus scoring technique.

6. When the leader is confident that the scorers for that question will apply the criteria consistently and accurately, the actual scoring begins.

Quality-control processes

A number of procedures are followed to ensure that accuracy of scoring is maintained during the scoring session. Most importantly, each response is scored twice, with the first scorer's decision hidden from the second scorer. If the two scores for a paper are the same or differ by only one point, the scoring for that paper is considered complete, and the test taker will be awarded the sum of the two scores. If the two scores differ by more than one point, the response is scored by a scoring leader, who has not seen the decisions made by the other two scorers. If this third score is midway between the first two scores, the test taker's score for the question is the sum of the first two ratings; otherwise, it is the sum of the third score and whichever of the first two scores is closer to it.

Another way of maintaining scoring accuracy is through "back-reading." Throughout the session, the leader for each question checks random samples of scores awarded by all the scorers. If the leader finds that a scorer is not applying the scoring criteria appropriately, that scorer is given more training.

At the beginning of the second day of reading, additional sets of papers are scored using the consensus method described above. This helps ensure that the scorers are refreshed on the scoring criteria and are applying them consistently.

Finally, the scoring session is designed so that several different scorers (usually four) contribute to any single test taker's score. This minimizes the effects of a scorer who might score slightly more harshly or generously than other scorers.

The entire scoring process—general and specific scoring guides, standardized benchmarks and samples, consensus scoring, adjudication procedures, back-reading, and rotation of exams to a variety of scorers—is applied consistently and systematically at every scoring session to ensure comparable scores for each administration and across all administrations of the test.

Advice from the Experts

Scorers who have scored thousands of real tests indicate the following practical pieces of advice.

1. **Read and answer the question accurately.**

   Be sure to dissect the parts of the question and analyze what each part is asking you to do. If the question asks you to "describe" or "discuss," keep those requirements in mind when composing your response—do not just give a list.

2. **Answer everything that is being asked in the question.**

   This seems simple, but many test takers fail to provide a complete response. If a question asks you to do three distinct things in your response, don't give a response to just two of those things. No matter how well you write about those two things, the scorers will not award you full credit.

3. **Give a thorough and detailed response.**

   Your response must indicate to the scorers that you have a thorough understanding of the applicable physical education principles and guidelines. The scorers will not read into your response. If something is not written, they do not know that you know it and will not give you credit for it.

4. **Do not change the question or challenge the basis of the question.**

   Stay focused on the question that is asked. You will receive no credit if you choose to answer another question or indicate that what the question is asking is inappropriate.

General Scoring Guide

Physical Education: Movement Forms—Analysis and Design (0092)

The following guide provides the framework for scoring the constructed-response questions on the *Analysis and Design* test.

Since each question in this test consists of several parts, a test taker's response is scored by rating each part individually. All parts are scored according to the scoring guide below, on a scale of 0–3.

One of the questions on the test always contains five parts. For this question, the total number of points that a response can receive from each scorer is 15. There are six parts to the other question on the test. For this question, the total number of points that a response can receive from each scorer is 18.

Score	Comment
3	Demonstrates a strong understanding of the principles of physical education and their appropriate application
2	Demonstrates an adequate understanding of the principles of physical education and their appropriate application
1	Demonstrates very little understanding of the principles of physical education and their appropriate application
0	Demonstrates no understanding of the principles of physical education or their appropriate application

General Scoring Guide

Physical Education: Movement Forms—Video Evaluation (0093)

The following guide provides the framework for scoring the constructed-response questions on the *Video Evaluation* test.

Each of the two questions is given a single score, on a scale of 0–6. The response is considered in its entirety when the scorer assigns the score.

Score	Comment
6	Demonstrates a superior understanding of the principles of physical education and their appropriate application
	Responds appropriately to all parts of the question
	Uses data provided in the question very accurately and effectively
	Provides very accurate, well-chosen, and well-developed descriptions of physical education activities
5	Demonstrates a strong understanding of the principles of physical education and their appropriate application
	Responds appropriately to all or nearly all parts of the question
	Uses data provided in the question accurately and effectively
	Provides accurate, well-chosen, and well-developed descriptions of physical education activities

Score	Comment	Score	Comment
4	Demonstrates an adequate understanding of the principles of physical education and their appropriate application	2	Demonstrates limited understanding, and may show some misunderstanding, of the principles of physical education and their appropriate application
	Responds appropriately to at least most parts of the question		May respond appropriately to only a few parts of the question
	Uses some data provided in the question fairly accurately and effectively		May use data provided in the question only in a very limited, inaccurate, and/or vague way
	Provides fairly accurate, well-chosen, and well-developed descriptions of physical education activities		Provides descriptions of physical education activities, but they may be seriously deficient in relevance, accuracy, and/or development
3	Demonstrates some understanding of the principles of physical education and their appropriate application	1	Demonstrates little or no understanding, and may show serious misunderstanding, of the principles of physical education and their appropriate application
	Responds appropriately to some parts of the question		May fail to respond appropriately to any part of the question
	Uses data provided in the question, but may show some inaccuracy and/or vagueness in use of data		May show serious inaccuracy and/or vagueness in use of data provided in the question, or may fail entirely to use such data
	Provides descriptions of physical education activities, but they may be somewhat deficient in relevance, accuracy, and/or development		May fail to provide descriptions of physical education activities, or may provide descriptions that are seriously flawed in relevance, accuracy, and/or development
		0	Blank, off-topic, or merely a restatement of the question

Question-Specific Scoring Guides

After a question is developed, three or four knowledgeable experts develop ideas for "model answers." These model answers are used to develop a Question-Specific Scoring Guide that creates a list of specific examples that would receive various scores. This list contains examples of various answers, not all possible answers. These question-specific scoring guides, which are based on model answers, provide the basis for choosing the papers that serve as the benchmarks and sample papers used for training the scorers at the scoring session. During the scoring sessions, specific examples can be added to the scoring guide, and papers can be added as samples for future readings.

Given the above information about how constructed-responses are scored and what the scorers are looking for in successful responses, you are now ready to look at specific questions, suggestions of how to approach the questions, and sample responses and scores given to those responses.

Chapter 8

Preparing for the *Physical Education: Movement Forms—Analysis and Design* Test

▶ ▶ ▶ ▶ ▶ ▶ ▶ ▶ ▶ ▶ ▶ ▶

The goal of this chapter is to provide you with strategies for how to read, analyze, and understand the questions on the *Movement Forms—Analysis and Design* test in physical education and then how to outline and write successful responses.

Introduction to the Question Types

The *Movement Forms—Analysis and Design* test in physical education is intended to assess how well a prospective teacher of physical education can select activities for particular purposes, make decisions about the status and needs of students, and provide explanations for those selections and decisions.

The test is composed of two constructed-response questions.

One question is formulated to evaluate your knowledge of psychomotor skills and your ability to design appropriate movement experiences for a range of age/ability levels (young children through 15-year olds) for a particular skill. Descriptions of four individuals of different age/ability levels are provided for this question.

The second question is formulated to evaluate your knowledge of using fitness assessment scores and your ability to design appropriate fitness programs based on assessment scores for a particular fitness component. A table indicating fitness scores for four individuals is provided for this question.

Each of the two questions also has a section that is designed to evaluate your understanding and application of basic principles of physical education.

What to Study

Success on this test is not simply a matter of learning more about how to respond to constructed-response questions. Success on the test also requires real knowledge of the field. As mentioned above, the test evaluates your ability to utilize fitness assessment scores to design appropriate fitness programs. The test is also designed to gather evidence about your knowledge of psychomotor skills and your ability to design appropriate movement activities.

It therefore would serve you well to read books and review notes in the areas of motor learning, motor development, exercise physiology, biomechanics, and descriptions of psychomotor skills.

The following books and Web sites are particularly relevant to the types of knowledge and ability covered by the test. **Note:** The test is not based on these resources, and they do not necessarily cover every topic that may be included in the test.

AAHPERD, *Physical Best Activity Guide—Elementary Level*. Human Kinetics, 1999.

This book provides an overview of fitness concepts and developmentally appropriate activities for children in elementary school.

AAHPERD, *Physical Best Activity Guide—Secondary Level*. Human Kinetics, 1999.

This book provides an overview of fitness concepts and fitness activities for individuals in middle school and high school.

Corbin, Charles, Ruth Lindsey, and Greg Welk. *Concepts of Fitness and Wellness*, 4th ed. McGraw-Hill, 2002.

This book provides an overview of fitness concepts and appropriate fitness exercises for all of the health-related fitness components. Contraindicated exercises are also described, and problems with the exercises are discussed.

Gallahue, David, and John Ozum. *Understanding Motor Development*, 4th ed. McGraw-Hill, 1998.

This book provides motor development theories and developmental stages for basic fundamental movement skills.

Human Kinetics, *Steps to Success Activity Series*, 2nd ed. 1995-1997.

This book provides descriptions of a wide variety of psychomotor skills.

Mood, Dale, Frank Musker, and Judith Rink. *Sports and Recreational Activities*, 11th ed. McGraw-Hill, 1995.

This series of books provides descriptions of a wide variety of psychomotor skills.

Nichols, Beverly. *Moving and Learning*, 3rd ed. Mosby, 1994.

This book provides developmentally appropriate activities for elementary school-age children and descriptions for psychomotor skills.

Rink, Judith. *Teaching Physical Education for Learning*, 2nd. ed. McGraw-Hill, 1993.

This book provides concepts in motor learning, a structure for developing an analysis of skills, and the process of developing a progression for learning a skill.

Schmidt, Richard, and Craig Wrisberg. *Motor Learning and Performance*, 2nd ed. Human Kinetics, 2000.

   This book provides information related to motor learning theories.

www.cooperinst.org

   This Web site gives an overview of the FITNESSGRAM and reference articles related to fitness.

http://pe.central.vt.edu/preschool/preschoolresources.html

   This Web site gives an extensive annotated reference list of developmentally appropriate physical education resources.

Understanding What the Questions Are Asking

It is impossible to write a successful response to a question unless you thoroughly understand the question. Often test takers jump into their written response without taking enough time to analyze exactly what the question is asking, how many different parts of the question need to be addressed, and how the information in the accompanying charts or tables needs to be addressed. The time you invest in making sure you understand what the question is asking will very likely pay off in a better performance, as long as you budget your time and do not spend a large proportion of the available time just reading the question.

To illustrate the importance of understanding the question before you begin writing, let's start with a sample question:

The FITNESSGRAM health-related fitness test battery includes the BACK-SAVER SIT-AND-REACH. The two tables printed below indicate the HEALTHY FITNESS ZONE for four individual boys or girls for the indicated test and the individual's score on the test.

	BACK-SAVER SIT-AND-REACH		
Parts	INDIVIDUAL AND AGE	HEALTHY FITNESS ZONE	INDIVIDUAL'S SCORE
I.	6-year-old boy	9 inches	6 inches
II.	10-year-old boy	8 inches	6 inches
III.	13-year-old girl	8 inches	8 inches
IV.	16-year-old girl	12 inches	6 inches

For <u>each</u> of the four individuals whose scores are given in the table, describe a safe and effective six-week program of exercises that the individual could engage in to improve in the BACK-SAVER SIT-AND-REACH, or to maintain fitness if the individual's score is already in the Healthy Fitness Zone. The exercise programs should be appropriate to age and developmental level of the individuals for whom they are recommended, and should also be appropriate for the level of fitness indicated by the individual's score.

V. Identify one principle of <u>motor learning</u>, <u>motor development</u>, <u>exercise physiology</u>, or <u>biomechanics</u> that can be used to justify or explain some aspect of one or more of the recommended exercise programs. Explain how this principle justifies or explains that aspect of the program or programs.

Key Components of the Question

✔ There are *five parts* to the question.

✔ For Parts I through IV, a program for *each* of the four individuals needs to be developed and *described*.

✔ Each program needs to be *six weeks* in length.

✔ Each program needs to be *safe*—it does not have the potential of causing harm to the individual.

✔ Each program needs to be *effective*—it will improve or maintain the individual's fitness level, as appropriate.

✔ Each program needs to show *recognition* of the *individual's fitness level* based on that individual's *test score*.

✔ For Part V, one of the areas of motor learning, motor development, exercise physiology, or biomechanics *needs to be selected*.

✔ *One principle*, which must come from the selected area, *needs to be identified*.

✔ The principle *needs to be able to be used to justify or explain* some *aspect* of the *exercise program or programs*.

✔ There needs to be an *explanation* of *how the principle justifies or explains* the particular *aspect* of the program or programs.

Organizing Your Response

Successful responses start with successful planning, either with an outline or with another form of notes. By planning your response, you greatly decrease the chances that you will forget to answer any part of the question. You increase the chances of creating a well-organized response, which is something the scorers look for. Your note-taking space also gives you a place to jot down thoughts whenever you think of them—for example, if you have an idea about one part of the question when you are writing your response to another part. Like taking time to make sure you understand what the question is asking, planning your response is time well invested, although you must keep your eye on the clock so that you leave sufficient time to write your response.

To illustrate a possible strategy for planning a response, let us focus again on the sample question introduced in the previous section. We analyzed the question and found that it necessitated a five-part response. You might begin by jotting down those parts on your notes page, leaving space under each. This will ensure that you address each part when you begin writing.

Sample Notes—Main Parts to Be Answered

I. Program for 6-year-old girl

II. Program for 10-year-old boy

III. Program for 13-year-old boy

IV. Program for 16-year-old girl

V. Principle

You then might quickly fill out the main ideas you want to address in each part, like this:

Sample Notes—Ideas Under Each Main Part

I. Program for 6-year-old girl

Variety of flexibility activities appropriate for 6 year old—with descriptions

6-week program

Indicate Frequency, Intensity, Time throughout program

II. Program for 10-year-old boy

Variety of flexibility activities appropriate for 10 year old—with descriptions

6-week program

Indicate Frequency, Intensity, Time throughout program

III. Program for 13-year-old boy

Appropriate flexibility activities for a 13-year old boy—with descriptions

6-week program

Indicate Frequency, Intensity, Time throughout program

IV. Program for 16-year-old girl

Appropriate flexibility activities for a 16-year old girl—with descriptions

6-week program

Indicate Frequency, Intensity, Time throughout program

V. Principle

Specifically identify a principle

Discuss principle related to the exercise programs

There are key characteristics that the scorers will look for:

- Answer all parts of the question.

- Give reasons for your answers.

- Demonstrate subject-specific knowledge in your answer.

- Refer to the data in the stimulus.

Now look at your notes and add any ideas that would address these characteristics. Notice below the additions that are made.

Sample Notes, with Added Ideas

I. Program for 6-year-old girl

Appropriate starting point—Refer to her score

Variety of flexibility activities appropriate for 6
year old—with descriptions

6-week program

*Show progression in Frequency, Intensity, and/or
Time throughout program*

II. Program for 10-year-old boy

Appropriate starting point—Refer to his score

Variety of flexibility activities appropriate for 10 year old—with
descriptions

6-week program

*Show progression in Frequency, Intensity, and/or
Time throughout program*

III. Program for 13-year-old boy

Appropriate starting point—Refer to his score

Appropriate flexibility activities for a 13-year old—
with descriptions

6-week program

*Show progression in Frequency, Intensity, and/or
Time throughout program*

IV. Program for 16-year-old girl

Appropriate starting point—Refer to her score

Appropriate flexibility activities for a 16-year old—with descriptions

6-week program

Show progression in Frequency, Intensity, and/or Time throughout program

V. Principle

Indicate one of the areas

Specifically identify a principle from this area

Discuss principle related to the exercise programs

You have now created the skeleton of your written response.

Writing Your Response

Now the important step of writing your response begins. The scorers will not consider your notes when they score your paper, so it is crucial that you integrate all the important ideas from your notes into your actual written response.

Some test takers believe that every written response on a Praxis test has to be in formal essay form— that is, with an introductory paragraph, then paragraphs with the response to the question, then a concluding paragraph. This is the case for very few Praxis tests (e.g., *English* and *Writing*). The *Movement Forms—Analysis and Design* test in physical education does **not** require formal essays, so you should use techniques that allow you to communicate information efficiently and clearly. For example, you can use bulleted or numbered lists, or a chart, or a combination of essay and chart.

Returning to our sample question, see below how the outline of the response to the first part of the question can become the final written response (this is an actual response by a test taker).

6-year-old girl—scored 6 in. and the healthy fitness zone is 9 in. She needs to improve in this area.

The following exercises will be used for this student:

When doing each of the exercises, the student should get into the exercise position, feel a slight stretch, and then slightly back off the stretch, and hold the stretch for the appropriate time. As the student goes through the six weeks, flexibility will increase and their distance per stretch will increase. It is important to do static stretching (holding the stretch) rather than ballistic stretching (bouncing into the stretch— No Bouncing.

Exercise #1—sitting stretch with legs out in front, knees slightly bent. Bend forward, reaching toward toes.

Exercise #2—sit with one leg extended out, knee slightly bent. Foot of opposite leg is brought in so that the bottom of the foot is touching the inside of the outstretched thigh. Reach forward toward the extended leg as far as possible. Repeat with legs in reverse position.

Wk 1—she will do both of the 2 exercises 3 times per week. She will hold each stretch for 8 secs.

Wk 2—both exercises 3 times per week. She will hold each stretch for 10 secs.

Wk 3—both exercises 4 times per week. Hold each 12 secs.

Wk 4—both exercises 4 times per week. Hold each 15 secs.

Wk 5—both exercises 5 times per week. Hold each 20 secs.

Wk 6—both 5 times per week. Hold each 25 secs.

While a chart may be appropriate for responding to the first four parts of the question, a discussion response is more appropriate for the last part of the question. Below is a sample response to the final part of the question—again, an actual response by a test taker—based on the outline created in the previous section.

The exercise physiology principle of specificity is being used throughout all of the exercise programs. In the area of flexibility, the principle of specificity indicates that flexibility is joint-specific—meaning that the specific area of the body must be stretched to increase flexibility. The two exercises that have been selected for all of the exercise programs help to increase flexibility in the hamstrings and the lower back area—which are the areas that are being measured in the Back-Saver Sit-and-Reach.

Whatever format you select, the important thing is that your answer needs to be thorough, complete, and detailed. You need to be certain that you do the following:

- Answer all parts of the question.

- Give reasons for your answers.

- Demonstrate subject-specific knowledge in your answer.

- Refer to the data in the stimulus.

Chapter 9

Practice Test, *Physical Education: Movement Forms—Analysis and Design*

▶   ▶   ▶   ▶   ▶   ▶   ▶   ▶   ▶   ▶   ▶   ▶

Now that you have worked through strategies and preparation relating to the *Physical Education: Movement Forms—Analysis and Design* test, you should take the following practice test. This test is an actual Praxis test, now retired. You will probably find it helpful to simulate actual testing conditions, giving yourself 60 minutes to work on the questions. You can use the lined answer pages provided if you wish.

Keep in mind that the test you take at an actual administration will have different questions. You should not expect your level of performance to be exactly the same as when you take the test at an actual administration, since numerous factors affect a person's performance in any given testing situation.

When you have finished the practice questions, you can read through the sample responses with scorer annotations in chapter 10.

Educational
Testing Service

TEST NAME:

Physical Education: Movement Forms—Analysis and Design (0092)

Time—60 Minutes

2 Questions

Question 1

The FITNESSGRAM health-related fitness test battery includes **the one-mile run/walk**. The table below indicates the HEALTHY FITNESS ZONE for four individual boys and girls for the one-mile run/walk and the individual's score on the test.

	ONE-MILE RUN/WALK		
Parts	INDIVIDUAL AND AGE	HEALTHY FITNESS ZONE	INDIVIDUAL'S SCORE
I.	6-year-old boy	Completion of distance	Completed 1/2 mile
II.	10-year-old boy	11:30-9:00	10:30
III.	13-year-old girl	11:30-9:00	11:00
IV.	16-year-old girl	10:00-8:00	12:00

For <u>each</u> of the four individuals whose scores are given in the table, describe a safe and effective six-week program of exercises that the individual could engage in to improve his or her performance in the one-mile run/walk or to maintain fitness if the individual's score is already in the Healthy Fitness Zone. The exercise programs should be appropriate to the age and the developmental level of the individuals for whom they are recommended and should also be appropriate for the level of fitness indicated by the individual's score.

V. Identify one principle of <u>motor learning</u>, <u>motor development</u>, <u>exercise physiology</u>, or <u>biomechanics</u> that can be used to justify or explain some aspect of one or more of the recommended exercise programs. Explain how this principle justifies or explains that aspect of the program or programs.

NOTES

Question 2

Choose <u>one</u> of the skills listed below.

- Basketball: dribbling

- Softball: batting

- Dance: performing a creative dance routine

Parts

I.   Describe 3–5 critical elements of the skill you have chosen.

II.   Describe an activity that is appropriate for 15-year-old boys and girls who are proficient in this skill. Your description of the activity should show how it would provide the opportunity for the participants to demonstrate mastery of the critical elements you described in Part I.

III.   Describe an activity that is appropriate for 12-year-old boys and girls who are familiar with this skill but not yet proficient in it. Your description of the activity should show how it would enable the participants to improve their mastery of one of the critical elements you described in Part I.

IV.   Describe an activity that is appropriate for 8-year-old boys and girls who have little or no experience with the skill. Your description of the activity should show how it would prepare participants to learn one of the critical elements you described in Part I.

V.   Describe an activity that is appropriate for 5- to 6-year-old boys and girls who have little or no experience with the skill. This activity should be of a general or fundamental nature and should not be specifically related to the skill you are addressing. Your description of the activity should show how it would prepare participants for the activity you described in Part IV.

VI.   Identify one principle of <u>motor learning</u>, <u>motor development</u>, <u>exercise physiology</u>, or <u>biomechanics</u> that can contribute toward justifying or explaining some aspect of one or more of the activities you have described in response to Parts II–V, and show how that principle justifies and/or explains that aspect of the activity or activities.

NOTES

Begin your response to Question 1 here.

_____

_____

_____

_____

_____

_____

_____

_____

_____

_____

_____

_____

_____

_____

_____

_____

_____

_____

_____

(Question 1 continued)

(Question 1 continued)

(Question 1 continued)

_____

_____

_____

_____

_____

_____

_____

_____

_____

_____

_____

_____

_____

_____

_____

_____

_____

_____

_____

_____

(Question 1 continued)

Begin your response to Question 2 here.

_____

_____

_____

_____

_____

_____

_____

_____

_____

_____

_____

_____

_____

_____

_____

_____

_____

_____

(Question 2 continued)

(Question 2 continued)

_____

_____

_____

_____

_____

_____

_____

_____

_____

_____

_____

_____

_____

_____

_____

_____

_____

_____

_____

(Question 2 continued)

(Question 2 continued)

_____

_____

_____

_____

_____

_____

_____

_____

_____

_____

_____

_____

_____

_____

_____

_____

_____

_____

_____

_____

_____

Chapter 10

Sample Responses and How They Were Scored, *Physical Education: Movement Forms—Analysis and Design*

▶ ▶ ▶ ▶ ▶ ▶ ▶ ▶ ▶ ▶ ▶ ▶

This chapter presents actual sample responses to the questions in the practice test and explanations for the scores they received.

As discussed in chapter 7, each question on the *Analysis and Design* test is scored in parts: each part is scored on a scale from 0 to 3. The general scoring guide used to score these parts is reprinted here for your convenience. There are five parts to Question 1: the total number of points that a response can receive from each scorer is 15. There are six parts to Question 2: the total number of points that a response can receive from each scorer is 18.

<u>Score</u>	<u>Comment</u>
3	Demonstrates a strong understanding of the principles of physical education and their appropriate application
2	Demonstrates an adequate understanding of the principles of physical education and their appropriate application
1	Demonstrates very little understanding of the principles of physical education and their appropriate application
0	Demonstrates no understanding of the principles of physical education or their appropriate application

Question 1

We will now look at four actual responses to Question 1 and see how the scoring guide above was used to rate each response.

Sample 1: Total Score of 9 (out of a possible 15)

1. 6 yr. old boy

- Week #1
  Run/Walk 1/2 mile   →   On first day, time the boy to see how long it
  *Teacher will run/walk with student   takes. This will help you see if he is
                                                        improving. Time each day. Challenge student
                                                        to decrease time.

  Homework   →   student will run/walk 10 minutes every
                                    afternoon after school

- Week #2
  Run/Walk 1/2 mile   →   Teacher will continue timing child

  P.E. class   →   Game—"Fitness Kickball" (high-intensity that requires a lot of running both on offense and defense). Jump rope 5 min.

  Homework   →   After school—run/walk for 12 min.

- Week #3
  Run/Walk 3/4 mile   →   Although time is not in consideration for his age, still continue using the stop watch. This will help motivate the student to improve.

  Homework   →   After school—run/walk for 14 min

- Week #4
  Run/Walk 3/4 mile in P.E.

  P.E. class   →   Game—"Get Fit with Frisbee" Jump rope at end of class for 5 min

  Homework   →   After school—run/walk for 15 min

- Week #5
  Run/Walk 1 mile (still using time for motivational purposes only)

  P.E. class   →   5 min. jump rope
  Practice Soccer Skills
  Activities: Partner follow the leader
  Course around cones

  Homework   →   Run/Walk for 15min

- Week #6
  Run/Walk 1 mile

  P.E. class   →   5 min. jump rope
  Run challenge course 2 times.
  Whip it activities—throw and retrieve

II. 10 yr. old boy (within fitness zone)

- **Week #1 & 2**

  Run/Walk 1 mile (still using time for motivational purposes only)

P.E. class	→	Run 2 laps around track
		Fitness Kickball
		Jump rope—5 min.
		1 time through challenge course
Homework	→	Run for 10 min after school

- **Week #3 & 4**

P.E. class	→	Run 3 laps around track
		Soccer skills—Focus on dribbling
		Partner follow leader
		Game Line Soccer
		Jump Rope (5 min.)

- **Week #5 & 6**

P.E. class	→	3 laps around track
		Play activities similar to speedball (variations)
		2 times through challenge course

III. 13 yr. old girl

- **Week #1–3**

  Run 3 laps at beginning of class (time run) try to decr. time

  Fitness kickball (wk. #1), soccer activities (wk #2 & 3)

  Jump rope 5 min. (end of class)

  Run/Walk for 12 min. after school

- **Week #4–6**

  Run/Walk 1 mile (time each run try to decr. time)

  Track & Field Unit—Do activities from various events—sprints, hurdles, distances, etc.)

  Jump Rope 5 min.

  Run/Walk for 15 min. after school

IV. 16 yr. old girl

- **Week #1 & 2**

  Run 2 laps, Walk 1 (beginning of class)

  Soccer Unit—variations of game; dribbling

  Jump Rope 5 min.

  Homework—Run/Walk 12 min. after school

- **Week # 3& 4**

  Run 2 laps, walk 1 run, Run 1 lap (beginning of class—time all mentioned for total)

  Track & Field Unit (see 13 yr. girl)

  Jump Rope 5–7 min.

  Homework—15 min. run/walk

- **Week #5 & 6**

  Run 3 laps, Walk 1 lap, Run 1 lap (time all laps)

  Aerobic Dance Unit

  Various high-intensity workouts

  Homework—15 min. run/walk

V.

Whole—part Progression

Breaking down of the entire mile into parts

For ex. Run 2 laps—Walk 1

This can help the student gradually reach his/her goal

Motivational Materials

By timing the students, you can set specific goals. Students love to achieve and meet their goals. It is important to set realistic goals.

Transfer Learning

By playing games that involve a great deal of running/walking, the students are getting exercise without realizing it.

Commentary on Sample 1:

I. **6-year-old boy**   Score of 2

The answer provided some variety of age-appropriate C-V activities—not just running. Increase in time (distance) was indicated. No frequency indicated.

II. **10-year-old boy**   Score of 2

The answer provided some variety of age-appropriate C-V activities—not just running. Increase in time (distance) was indicated. No frequency indicated.

III. **13-year-old girl**   Score of 2

The answer provided variety of C-V activities. Some increase in time was indicated. No frequency indicated.

IV. **16-year-old girl**   Score of 2

The answer provided variety of C-V activities. Some increase in time and intensity was indicated. No frequency indicated.

V. **Principle**   Score of 1

Two principles were named. The area the principles related to was not identified. The discussion of the principles was not correct.

Sample 2: Total Score of 8 (out of a possible 15)

I-IV

I. **Wk. #1** Work on completing 1/2 mile distance at a walk—Keep track of laps and distance on a record sheet. exercise 3 days out of the week, other 2 days participate in "other" physical activities that promote general fitness.

Wk #2 Work on completing 1/2 mile distance at a walk, begin to keep time records for the boy. Although this is not required of the FITNESSGRAM, it will allow the boy a "picture" and feeling of improvement and success where he sees improvement.

Wk #3 Work on increasing distance of 3/4 walk. Keep track of improvements in distance, add to log 2 days out of the week, remaining 2 days other fitness activities.

Wk #4 Keep times of 3/4 distance. Write improvements in log work on completing 3/4 distance 3 days out of the week.

Wk #5 Work on completing 1 mile at a walk, write down distance improvements in log 3 days out of the week, other 2 days = general fitness activities.

Wk #6 Keep time improvement of 1 mile distance in log, the boy can compare improvements from wk #1 and how he feels about his success.

II. Wk #1 3 days out of the week jog 1/2 mile, walk 1/2 mile. 2 days out of the week participate in "general fitness" activities.

Wk #2 jog 1 lap, walk 1 lap for 1 mile. 3 days out of the week, other 2 days "general fitness activities."

Wk #3 Jog 1 lap, walk 1 lap, mark times on performance in a log. 3 days out of the week— remaining 2 days general fitness participation.

Wk #4 Jog 1 lap, walk 1 lap, continue to mark times in log. At end of the week, should see some time improvements 2 days general fitness activities

Wk #5 Jog 3/4 mile, walk 1/4 mile, note times in log. 3 days out of the week. 2 remaining days "general fitness activities".

Wk #6 Complete 1 mile as best as they can note times in log. End of the week compare time improvements from initial test score.

III. Basically same type of structure as II (10 year old boy).

	Intensity	Time (duration)	Distance
Wk #1	Jog/Walk (alternate lap)	any time	1 ml.
Wk #2	Jog 1/2 ml walk 1/2 ml	note time	1 ml
Wk #3	Jog/walk (alternate laps)	note time	1 ml
Wk #4	Jog 1/2 ml/walk 1/4 ml	note time	1 ml
Wk #5	Jog 3/4 ml/walk 1/4 ml.	anytime	1 ml
Wk #6	Finish Distance at best	note time	1 ml

End of the week discuss time improvements from initial test time.

IV.

Wk #1	Jog/walk (alternate lap)	anytime	1 ml
Wk #2	Jog/walk (alternate lap)	record time	1 ml
Wk #3	Jog/Walk (1/2 ml alternate)	any time	1 ml
Wk #4	Jog/Walk 1/2 ml alternate)	record time	1 ml
Wk #5	Jog/Walk best	anytime	1 ml
Wk #6	Jog/Walk best	record time	1 ml

Note improvements in times so student sees improvement & builds confidence.

V.

Runners/students can keep/monitor heart rates during bouts of exercise, to make sure they are staying within 60–80% of their Maximum Heart Rate—maintaining optimum cardiovascular training. They should see improvements with their times/distance compared to heart beats per minute as well (Exercise Physiology).

The exercise programs are built upon a basic overload training principle that is appropriate overloading/training without becoming aerobic in training. Building upon the previous effort.

Commentary on Sample 2:

I.   **6-year-old boy**   Score of 1

The answer did have a six-week program that indicated frequency and progression for time (distance) and intensity. However, this response did not indicate developmentally appropriate activities. The response indicated the 6-year-old child would do only distance work. By week 5, the child would be completing 1 mile three times a week.

II.   **10-year-old boy**   Score of 1

The answer did have a six-week program that indicated frequency and progression for time (distance) and intensity. However, this response did not indicate developmentally appropriate activities. The response indicated the 10-year-old child would do only distance work. Throughout the program, the child would be completing 1 mile three times a week.

III.   **13-year-old girl**   Score of 2

A six-week program is indicated. Jog/walk activity is only adequate for this developmental level. Some increase in intensity was indicated. Frequency needed to be assumed, because of the reference to Part II.

IV.   **16-year-old girl**   Score of 2

A six-week program is indicated. Jog/walk activity is only adequate for this developmental level. Some increase in intensity was indicated. Frequency was not indicated.

V.   **Principle**   Score of 2

The answer talked somewhat about target heart rate and the overload principle—both related to exercise physiology. The response did not develop how either principle was utilized in any of the programs.

Sample 3: Total Score of 8 (out of a possible 15)

According to research conducted by Amer. Med. Ass. all from 2 yrs. of age should be active for 30 min. daily.

CA State Phys. Fitness Standards   6 wk lesson plan for 6 yr. old Boy

Objective—The student will be able to engage in phys. activity that causes increased heart rate and heavy breathing. Introductory Activities—TAG GAMES (2–3 min).

(FD) Fitness Development (7–8) min. abdominal muscular strength & endurance. Parachute fitness.

1. jog holding chute
2. curl-ups
3. skip holding chute
4. arm circles
5. hold chute a diff. levels
6. seat walk to ctr. of chute
7. jog in place—hold chute
8. bench-pull body forward
9. lie on back shake chute w/feet
10. sit & reach

Lesson Focus (15–20)—movement skills

Basketball skills—Dribbling—Dribble w/finger pads not slap

Bounce & catch 1x, 5x, 10x,—dominant hand & non-dominant

Dribble to music—L & Rt hand

Introduce Movement & Dribbling— walking, skipping, jogging

Game (5–7)

Blindfolded Duck

Closure: Ask ques.—How did you feel? How many times could you dribble w/out making a mistake?

F.I.T.

Frequency—5x per wk

Intensity—moderate

Time—30 min.

Wk #1—Pretest one mile run/walk; Fitness Development—20 sec.

Wk #2—FD—22 sec.

Wk #3—FD—25 sec.

Wk #4—FD—27 sec.

Wk #5—FD 30 sec.

Wk #6 Post test Day 1, Day 2-5 = FD 30 sec.

6 wk lesson—6 yr. old—the student should be able to complete the 1 mile walk run according to state phys. fitness standards.

10 yr. old

I. Introductory (2–3 min)—Bean Bag Touch & Go

(FD) II. Fitness Development—Hustle—Skip, jog, side step, hop

(CT) Circuit Training Hustle—hustle 25–45—Strength endurance 30–60 sec., 30–55 hustle

1. arm circles
   hustle

2. crunches
   hustle

3. shoulder stretch
   hustle

4. rope climb
   hustle

5. power jumps

6. arm curls—resistance bands
   hustle

7. military press—resistance bands
   hustle

8. curl-ups
   hustle

9. push-ups
   hustle

10. sit & reach

The objective: 1. The student will be able to move for a min. of 15. 2. The student will be able to meet the state phys. fitness standards of a fifth grader

Wk #1—Pretest—1 mile run, (FD) Day 2–5 hustle—25 sec.; strength & endurance—30 sec.

Wk #2 —Day 1–5 CT—30 sec., st & end. 35 sec.

Wk #3   "   35   "   "   40 sec.

Wk #4   "   40   "   "   45 sec.

Wk #5   "   45   "   "   50 sec.

Wk #6—Post Test—day 1—1 mile run Day 2–5 CT—50 sec. S&E—55

At the end of the 6 wk lesson the 10 yr. old should reduce the 1 mile time to 9:30

Lesson Focus (15–20 min)

Basketball Skills—

Review 1 hand set shot lay-up

Defending (guarding) Chest & Bounce Pass Two hand overhead Pass

Lead up—3 man Weave

Game (5–7 min—21 game

Closure—Did you understand the 3 man weave? Does everyone know what BEEF? <u>B</u>alance <u>E</u>yes on ball <u>E</u>lbow—90% <u>F</u>ollow Through

Demonstrate

13/16 yr. old girl—the objectives

1. The student will be able to design a personal health related fitness program.—13 yr/16 yr.

2. The student will be able to maintain physical activities at a target heart rate of 145–176—13 yr.

3. The student will be able to be physically active in a variety of phys. activities.

13/16 yr old.

Introductory Activities—warm-up—static stretch hold for 10–60 sec.
　　upper—shoulder stretch—arm circle
　　trunk—pretzel—side bend
　　lower—sit and reach—knee hug

Fitness Development (FD)—13 yr. 20 min　　　16 yr 30–60 min.

Weight Circuit Training CT　3x per week　　　3x per wk
　　　　　　　　　　　　　2 sets of 10　　　3 sets of 10

13 yr Cardio—Legs/13yr /16yr　　　　　　cardio—choose sport

leg extension　　　　　squats—3 of 10　　　　cycling

ham curls　　　　　　　　　　　　　　　　　jogging

lunges—w/weights　　　　　　　　　　　cross-country

calf raise—20 reps　　　　　　　　　　　track & field

leg press—20 reps introductory weight　　　　Skiing
　　　　whatever is comfortable　　　　　　Hiking
　　　　w/10 reps.　　　　　　　　　　　Football
　　　　Do not increase by more than　　　　Tennis
　　　　10% per wk.　　　　　　　　　Basketball
　　　　13/yr—16yr　　　　　　　　　　Soccer

13 yr old F.I.T → 2 sets of 10

Day 1 Pretest—1 mile run—running drills—5 x 25 yds

Day 2–5 CT

Day 3 Cardio—440 warm-up stretching legs—10 min.
　　　　　　　　progressive sprints—5x50 yds
　　　　　　　　2 laps warm down jog
　　　　　　　　stretch—23 min.

Day 2—CT Training & Cardio

Day 3—CT & Cardio

Wk #1—Pretest; Day 2 & 3—CT & Cardio

Wk #2 Day 1–3 CT & Cardio

Wk #3 Day 1–3 CT & Cardio

Wk #4 "   "

Wk #5 "   "

Wk #6—Post Test only; Day 2-3 CT & Cardio

At the end of six wks student will be able to run a 9:00 mile.

16 yr. old Standard 3→The student will be able to be physically active in a variety of phys. activities.

CARDIO—M,W,F CT—M,W,F Same—Cardio for 13 yr old plus choose sport for 30 min

Wk #1 Pretest—1 mile run Day 2–5 CT & Cardio CT & Cardio choose sport for 30 min.

Wk #2 Day 2-5 CT & Cardio for 13 yr. old sport for 35 min.

Wk #3   "   "   "   40 min

Wk #4   "   "   "   45 min

Wk #5   "   "   "   50 min

Wk #6 Post Test—1 mile run—Day 2–5 CT & Cardio for 55 min.

The student will be able to run a 8–9:00 mile

Exercise—Physiology - Target heart rate is calculated by

220-age x .70 = h-rate

220-age x .85 = h-rate

The 6 wk lesson plans are developmental appr. for their ages.

Commentary on Sample 3:

I.   6-year-old boy   Score of 2

The answer provided some indication of a six-week program. Some variety of developmentally appropriate activities was indicated. Some increase in time was indicated.

II.   10-year-old boy   Score of 2

The answer provided some indication of a six-week program. Some variety of developmentally appropriate activities was indicated. Some increase in time was indicated.

III.   13-year-old girl   Score of 1

The answer provided some indication of a six-week program. Specific activities for the program are not clear. No indication of progression through the six weeks.

IV.   16-year-old girl   Score of 1

The answer provided some indication of a six-week program. Specific activities for the program are not clear. Some indication of increase in "sport" time throughout program—not clearly explained.

V.   Principle   Score of 2

The answer indicated the calculation of the target heart rate (THR), related to the area of exercise physiology. No discussion was provided that related THR to any of the exercise programs.

Sample 4: Total Score of 5 (out of a possible 15)

I.   For the 6 year old boy I would start him off with elementary stretches like sit and reach, and hurdle stretch. I would recommend that the student begins each workout stretching to gain more flexibility. This is proven to improve physical fitness on all levels of exercise physiology. The student would then jog 4 laps around the gym to increase his heart rate. He will then do 2 sets of push-ups at 10 reps (adjust depending on endurance). The next exercise he will complete is 2 sets of 10 jumping jacks. He will then be responsible for 2 sets of 10 sit-ups or crunches. after these are completed he will be responsible for 8–10 mins. of walking or running. This is for the first 2 weeks and is to be done at least 3 times a week. After 2nd week you must re-evaluate the student. Expecting to increase each set of exercises by 5 reps each week after the 2nd. The student will be expected to run the entire 8 mins. of the 5th week.

II.   For the 10 year old I once again began workout by stretching. Use stretches that work upper and lower legs (3times wk) along with back & arms. Began with 3 sets of 8 push ups, followed by 3 sets of 10 sit-ups. The student will began his first two weeks finishing program by running/walking a mile. After 2nd week at 1/4 of mile to run/walk. After the 4th week add 1/2 mile to run/walk. Students need to increase # of sit-ups after each week. By putting more demand on the body each week your body will be able to adapt. These exercises are used to work on your bodies ATP supply. By putting this demand on body the supply will increase.

III. Began workout by stretching. Then have student jog for 3–5 mins (increasing by 30 sec. each week). Next have student do 2 sets of polymeric hops which will strengthen muscles and give them more power and flexibility. Finish workout with 5–8 min jog. Increase as student stamina increases.

IV. Began by having student walk for 3–5 min at fast pace, to get heart pumping. Next have student stretch out legs & arms. Next have student do jumping jacks 2 sets of 8. Last have student run/walk for 5–10 mins. After every lap student must climb a row of stairs (pref. in gym). Time will vary according to the students progress.

Commentary on Sample 4:

I. 6-year-old boy   Score of 1

Only the activities related to C-V development are evaluated. The activities related to flexibility and muscular strength and endurance are not considered in the evaluation. The answer indicated the child would only do distance work for C-V development. No progression over six weeks is indicated.

II. 10-year-old boy   Score of 1

Only the activities related to C-V development are evaluated. The activities related to flexibility and muscular strength and endurance are not considered in the evaluation. The answer indicated the child would only do distance work for C-V development. No progression over six weeks is indicated.

III. 13-year-old girl   Score of 1

Six-week program not actually indicated. Progression over six weeks not indicated. Did mention "jog" as an activity.

IV. 16-year-old girl   Score of 1

Six-week program not actually indicated. Progression over six weeks not indicated. Did mention "run/walk" as an activity.

V. Principle   Score of 1

Although not specifically labeled, recognition was given to the fact that ATP was mentioned in II.

Question 2

The same 0–3 scoring guide used for Question 1 is applied to each part of this question.

We will now look at five samples and see how the scoring guide was used to rate each part of the response.

Sample 5: Total Score of 12 (out of a possible 18)

Basketball dribbling

I. using finger pads/not palms
able to dribble with both hands & charge (crossover) over easily
head up
dribbling hard out to guard against defender

II. dribbling while being guarded by opponent back and forth down the court between two lines (object to not get the ball stolen)have the students shout out while dribbling the # on the flash card the teacher holds up @ the end of the court.
they must keep head up 2 read #'s arm up to keep it from being stolen, change hands to sc back & forth + "soft fingers" to make sure they're using their pads

III. Dribble stationary w/left hand then right (in own self space)
calling out names of words teacher holds up @ end of gym on cue cards/teacher blows whistle
students switch hand/teacher beats drum once
students move forward beats drum twice—student stop
here students would learn how 2 switch hands & keep head up → other 2 elements could be refined after these

IV. Dribbling in self space → drop ball w/2 hands, dribble once w/down hand & then catch & repeat → teaching cue → soft fingers—teacher emphasize dribbling w/finger pads → increase # of dribbles as proficiency increases/switch hand periodically.

V. With large balloons have the children bat them w/ both hands → See how long they can keep this up. Make up games like "hot potato" or pretend the balloon is a bomb getting ready 2 explode ← if it hits the ground.
then have them bat the ball w/one hand using only their finger tips (both hands)

4 hrs. will help develop one-hand coordination & also let them get the feel for using their finger pads not just their palms.

VI. In motor devel., the concept I would use to describe would be that of building on the basic fundamental skills and their increasing the difficulty. In #5 by starting out w/one dribble & then increasing the # of dribbles → student's get basic skill down → & get a kinesthetic awareness of it. From here they can continue 2 add on by dribbling more stationary, switch hands & then moving. But 1st they have to know what dribbling feels like & 2 use f. pads sc theses others might be easier. Must start @ foundations and build up (Break down the skill).

Commentary on Sample 5:

I.   Critical elements   Score of 2

Somewhat more than a list. Some attempt was made to describe.

II. 15 year olds   Score of 2

Activity somewhat appropriate. Some attempt to indicate demonstration of mastery of critical elements.

III. 12 year olds   Score of 2

A critical element is indicated. Some attempt to indicate how activity would improve mastery of a critical element.

IV. 8 year olds   Score of 2

One of the critical elements indicated. Some attempt at indicating how activity would prepare them to learn the critical element.

V.   5–6 year olds   Score of 2

Activity is fundamental in nature. Somewhat relates to activity for 8 year old.

VI. Principle   Score of 2

Did not identify a principle. Somewhat described a concept.

Sample 6: Total Score of 11 (out of a possible 18)

DANCE: Performing a creative dance routine

I. Elements
    (A) Basic Dance Steps
    (B) Timing
    (C) Locomotor/Nonlocomtor Movements
    (D) Creativity

II. 15 yr. boys & girls (Proficient)
    Activity ⟶ Groups of 4 or 5 (heterogenous)
    Create/choreograph dance routine for High School dance team. Each group has to have at least 40 counts in 4's or 8's and apply to appropriate music. Each group will be responsible for teaching the rest of the class on the group's assigned date. Evaluate on creativity, timing w/music, togetherness, steps, and use of at least 3 locomotor skills.

III. 12 yr. boys/girls (familiar)
    Activity ⟶ Groups of 4 or 5 (hetero)
    Line dancing—using basic dance steps and 2 locomotor skills each group will create a line dance. Remembering that line dancing repeats itself every time you change directions or run out of steps. You do not stop until the music stops. The students will use counts of 4 or 8 out loud to enhance timing. Each group will be give a day to perform. Teacher picks appropriate music (fast/slow) and attempt to teach others with help from teacher. Remind them simple is better!

IV. 8 year
    (A) Review basic flash cards with locomotor/nonloc. movements on each. Use music.
    (B) Teach Basic Dance Steps that are universal. (ex.) Grapevine, step-touch
    Teach a basic line dance. (ex.) Grape R, Grap L
    Step back R
    Step back L
    Step back R

L knee up to hop
Feet together (clap)
Repeat.

V. 5/6 yrs. old

(A) Freeze & move (timing)

1. When music plays create new ways to move or make different shapes, when music stops you must "Freeze".

Emphasize "hold" in dancing.

(B) Introduce Primary/Secondary Locomotor Skills.

1. Using a stack of cards with a skill on each, pull a cord (using diff. music fast/slow) Read it for those who can't and they must do it. Keep pulling a new skill every 5 to 7 seconds.

Establish personal space while doing skills to avoid collision.

* Around holidays utilize basic skills with music such as Easter → Bunny Hop. → Halloween → Martian Hop.

VI. Motor learning → Memory Principle

For each age level I have remembered short term & working memory capacities for each. Each activity is more complex the higher the age level. The 15 year olds can store more information and use association, therefore their task is the most difficult. The 5 & 6 year olds do not have as much success with difficulty, therefore simple and short with a lot of repetition will enhance their learning.

Commentary on Sample 6:

I. **Critical elements**   Score of 1

What is listed is correct. No descriptions are given.

II. **15 year olds**   Score of 2

Appropriate activity. Some attempt to indicate demonstration of mastery of critical elements.

III. **12 year olds**   Score of 2

Creativity is used in the activity. Line dancing is not considered creative dance.

IV. **8 year olds**   Score of 2

Basic locomotor movement to music is creative. Line dancing is not considered creative dance.

V. **5–6 year olds**   Score of 2

Activity is fundamental in nature. Activity seems to use creativity. Activity not developed completely.

VI. **Principle**   Score of 2

Described a principle in a basic way and somewhat related it to activities.

Sample 7: Total Score of 9 (out of a possible 18)

Dance:

15 year old boys & girls (proficient): The students have in previous classes learned & demonstrated special awareness, concentration, rhythm (even, uneven) (with & without music) & balance while performing the dances & dance steps. In the follow class (activity) the students will be given music & they are to come up with their own personal dance. They must incorporate most the steps (at least 5) that they learned in class. They must include balance (which could be shown by twisting or turns, rhythm (even uneven) & spatial (awareness). They will then at the end of the activity present to the class or if they choose me personally.

12 yr. boys & girls: The students have learned many basic dance steps & have seen & practiced them in 4 different dances. The student must choose one of the dances and pick their own music (from a selection) & show me that they can keep the correct rhythm. The emphasis is on rhythm & keeping the correct count.

8 yr—We would start with no music & we would count 1, 2, 3, 4. Then we would all walk to 1 (right) 2 (left) & so on. Then we would change the speed. We would then practice step hop. We would all count 1, 2, 3, 4& would go (1) step, (2) hop, (3) step, (4) hop. then we would learn (1) step, (2) step, (3) step, (4) hop. (Changing the speed count each time. Then we would add (slow) music. I would have students practice one dance step at a time then mix it up by my command. After they got familiar allow them to mix up all the steps.

5–6 yrs—Students will begin to count their steps. Have music playing in the background & they move around performing different task. The students will skip, hop, walk, run & so on. When the music stops they must be still. This activity gets students familiar with music & listening to the music. Also it exposes them to movement while music is playing. They also are counting their steps but there is no steady beat yet.

VI. Motor Development:

At these levels the students are either proficient or close to it. They are able to perform the skills on their own. With little or no help. The next logic step in MD is to have them create their own dance or music for a dance. This way they are being challenged within themselves & they are held accountable by teacher & piers.

Commentary on Sample 7:

I. **Critical elements**   Score of 1

Although not specifically indicated, recognition was given to the listing in the first part of the 15-year-olds activity.

II. **15 year olds**   Score of 2

Appropriate activity. Some attempt to indicate demonstration of mastery of critical elements.

III. **12 year olds**   Score of 2

A critical element was indicated. Appropriate activity. Some attempt at indicating how activity would improve mastery of a critical element.

IV. **8 year olds**   Score of 2

Appropriate activity. Some indication of a critical element. Some attempt at indicating how activity would prepare them to learn the critical element.

V.   5–6 year olds   Score of 2

Activity is fundamental in nature. Some attempt to relate to 8-year-olds activity.

VI.   Principle   Score of 0

Did not identify a principle. Did not describe or discuss a principle.

Sample 8: Total Score of 7 (out of a possible 18)

Softball batting

I.   accuracy/form/transfer of learning/force

II. 15 year old boys and girls who are proficient in this skill would benefit from participating in a game, I feel. They would demonstrate mastery of the skills in Part I by how they execute their turns at bat. For instance, do they strike out constantly? Do they hit fly balls constantly? Can they bunt? Do they need to adjust their stance or grip on the bat for better results?

III. 12 year old boys & girls may benefit from a modified game. 1) Hit off a tee but keep the rest of the rules of the game the same. After this goal has been accomplished engage in a regular game. or 2) modify the rules of the game (4 strikes, 4 outs, etc.) to allow for correction/practice of those specific elements in #1 that they are experiencing difficulty with. Another possibility would be to break them into smaller props (instead of 2 teams/sides) to allow for exploration/student-peer help.

IV. For 8 year olds—I would begin with a target game to work on accuracy and form 1st. I would explore/find activities for striking and hitting with either objects in other ways and then progress to hitting off a tee. After the tees I would progress to partners and tossing.

V.   5 and 6 year olds need to use different balls and different implements to strike with. I would start with throwing and catching—Progress to hitting off a tee (with larger implements and bat and then use a toss. Also—whoever was doing the tossing would stand closer than for a 15 year old who was hitting. I would explore/find games and activities similar to batting but not using batting until they had the basics down.

VI. A principle of motor learning which I think applies to softball batting is progression—from simple (general) to specifics. If a child/children cannot aim or move their bodies to throw and catch balls they will not be able to strike a ball The size of the ball needs to start large and progress smaller. As does the striking implements. Also, the way the ball is presented thrown, overhand, underhand, fast, tossed etc. has a bearing on the success of hitting.

Commentary on Sample 8:

I. Critical elements   Score of 1

What is listed is somewhat correct. No descriptions are given.

II. 15 year olds   Score of 1

There is an attempt to indicate basis for evaluating mastery. No relationship made to the critical elements indicated in I.

III. 12 year olds   Score of 1

Some description of an activity. No critical element identified.

IV. 8 year olds   Score of 1

Description of activity not clearly developed.

V. 5–6 year olds   Score of 1

Several ideas were indicated. No one activity was clearly described/developed.

VI. Principle   Score of 2

A principle of motor learning was identified and somewhat described. An attempt was made to relate the principle to an activity.

Sample 9: Total Score of 2 (out of a possible 18)

Softball—"batting"

I.
  - (1) stance
  - (2) grip of bat (hand position)
  - (3) swinging
  - (4) eye contact

II. 15 year old
  - (1) the girl should stand with her feet shoulders width apart and aligned with the plate etc.
    - —knees are with a slight bend
    - —back straight but torso tilted towards the plate ex:
    - —elbows should be bent a 90° angle (chest high).
  - (2) the bat should be held with one hand over the other with a small (1/4—1/2) inch from the end.
  - (3) bring bat in a back-ward move while shifting front foot forward then swing the bat around with arms fully extended.
  - (4) make sure you have good eye coordination and watch the ball all the way to the bat.

III. (12 year old)

The main problem a 12 year old may have is with swinging ex: drop his should when he swings.

He would need some practice swing over - and - over example maybe up close to a fence that has a line painted on it. He could watch the line and practice swings and this might help him.

Commentary on Sample 9:

I.   **Critical elements**   **Score of 1**

These are critical elements. No descriptions are given.

II.   **15 year olds**   **Score of 0**

An activity is not given. This is a description of the skill.

III. **12 year olds**   **Score of 1**

An activity is given. Description is not well developed.

IV.   **8 year olds**   **Score of 0**

No response given to this section.

V.   **5–6 year olds**   **Score of 0**

No response given to this section.

VI.   **Principle**   **Score of 0**

No response given to this section.

Chapter 11

Preparing for the *Physical Education: Movement Forms—Video Evaluation* Test

► ► ► ► ► ► ► ► ► ► ► ►

The goal of this section is to provide you with strategies for how to read, analyze, and understand the questions on the *Movement Forms—Video Evaluation* test in physical education and then how to outline and write successful responses.

Introduction to the Question Types

The *Movement Forms—Video Evaluation* test in physical education is designed to assess how well a prospective teacher of physical education can identify critical features in the performance of movement forms and exercises, and describe appropriate ways to communicate with individual performers about ways of changing and/or improving their performance. The test also assesses the ability of the prospective teacher of physical education to identify unsafe aspects of movement and exercise performance.

The test is composed of two constructed-response questions. Each question is based on a video (one to two minutes long) of school-age children performing various movements. The movements may include psychomotor skills or fitness exercises. The taped stimulus for each question shows two to six demonstrators performing the skill or exercise for that question. You may be asked to describe significant characteristics of the child's performance and suggest appropriate ways to improve that performance. You may be asked to identify errors with the execution of an exercise and to identify injuries resulting from those errors.

You will see the videos for both questions at the beginning of the test and will see each video four additional times during the hour.

What to Study

Success on this test is not simply a matter of learning more about how to respond to constructed-response questions. Success on the test also requires real knowledge of the field. As mentioned above, the test evaluates your ability to identify critical features in the performance of movement forms and exercises, and your ability to describe appropriate ways to communicate with individual performers about ways of changing and/or improving their performance. The test also evaluates your ability to identify errors of execution or unsafe aspects of exercises and to identify potential injuries from those errors.

It therefore would serve you well to read books and review notes in the areas of motor development, biomechanics, descriptions of psychomotor skills, qualitative analysis of skills, descriptions of fitness exercises, and contraindicated exercises.

The following books are particularly relevant to the types of knowledge and ability covered by the test. **Note:** The test is not based on these resources, and they do not necessarily cover every topic that may be included in the test.

Corbin, Charles, Ruth Lindsey, and Greg Welk. *Concepts of Fitness and Wellness*, 4th ed. McGraw-Hill, 2002.

This book provides an overview of fitness concepts and descriptions of appropriate fitness exercises for all of the health-related fitness components. Contraindicated exercises are also described, and problems with the exercises are discussed.

Gallahue, David, and John Ozum. *Understanding Motor Development*, 4th ed. McGraw Hill, 1998.

This book provides motor-development theories and developmental stages for basic fundamental movement skills.

Human Kinetics, *Steps to Success Activity Serie*s, 2nd ed., 1995–1997.

This series of books provides descriptions of a wide variety of psychomotor skills. Potential errors of performance are also presented.

Knudson, Duane, and Craig Morrison. *Qualitative Analysis of Human Movement*, 2nd ed. Human Kinetics, 2002.

This book provides an interdisciplinary model of qualitative analysis of human movement. Included with the book is an interactive CD-ROM that provides practice with analysis of motor performance and feedback about proper responses.

Mood, Dale, Frank Musker, and Judith Rink. *Sports and Recreational Activities*, 11th ed. McGraw-Hill, 1995.

This book provides descriptions of a wide variety of psychomotor skills.

Nichols, Beverly. *Moving and Learning*, 3rd ed. Mosby, 1994.

This book provides descriptions of psychomotor skills and fitness exercises.

Rink, Judith. *Teaching Physical Education for Learning*, 2nd. ed. McGraw Hill, 1993.

This book provides a structure for developing an analysis of skills, the process of developing a progression for learning a skill, and the development of cues related to each level of the progression.

Understanding What the Questions Are Asking

It is impossible to write a successful response to a question unless you thoroughly understand the question. Often test takers jump into their written response without taking enough time to analyze exactly what the question is asking, how many different parts of the question need to be addressed, and how the visual stimulus needs to be addressed. The time you invest in making sure you understand what the question is asking will very likely pay off in a better performance, as long as you budget your time and do not spend a large proportion of the available time just reading the question.

To illustrate the importance of understanding the question before you begin writing, let's start with a sample question:

Make specific reference to the performance of the two demonstrators (in this case, the demonstrators are boys) in the video in answering the following questions.

> **For each of the two demonstrators:**
>
> > **Describe the stage of development in the skill that the demonstrator's performance indicates.**
> >
> > **Describe two important features of that stage of development that are clearly visible in the demonstrator's performance on the tape.**
>
> **For one of the demonstrators:**
>
> > **Describe a verbal cue that you could give that demonstrator to help the demonstrator further develop proficiency in performing this skill. This cue should be appropriate to that demonstrator's stage of development in the skill and should be related to a feature of performance of the skill clearly visible in the video.**

The two demonstrators were instructed to slide to the right three times.

Key Components to the Question

✔ There are *three parts* to the question.

✔ *Each* of the *three parts* needs to be a description.

✔ For Part 1, a general description of the stage of development for *each* demonstrator needs to be provided. This should be a description of the attributes that are generally exhibited at that specific stage of development.

✔ For Part 2, *two* features presented in Part 1, which are seen in the video performance, should be described for *each* performer.

✔ For Part 3, a *verbal cue* should be described for one of the demonstrators. This cue should help the demonstrator develop proficiency of the skill, should be appropriate to the demonstrator's stage of development, and should be related to a feature clearly visible in the video.

Organizing Your Response

Successful responses start with successful planning, either with an outline or with another form of notes. By planning your response, you greatly decrease the chances that you will forget to answer any part of the question. You also increase the chances of creating a well-organized response, which is something the scorers look for. Your note-taking space also gives you a place to jot down thoughts whenever you think of them, for example, if you have an idea about one part of the question when you are writing your response to another part. Like taking time to make sure you understand what the question is asking, planning your response is time well invested, although you must keep your eye on the clock so that you have sufficient time to write your response.

To illustrate a possible strategy for planning a response, let us focus again on the sample question introduced in the previous section. We analyzed the question and found that it necessitated a three-part response. You might begin by jotting down those parts on your notes page, leaving space under each. This will ensure that you address each part when you begin writing.

Sample Notes—Main Parts to Be Answered

1. General description of stage of development for demonstrator #1

   General description of stage of development for demonstrator #2 (Select an acceptable framework for stages of development of motor skills.)

2. Description of two features seen in the video for demonstrator #1 that are part of the stage of development described in Part 1

   Description of two features seen in the video for demonstrator #2 that are part of the stage of development described in Part 1

3. For one of the demonstrators, a verbal cue needs to be described. The cue needs to be appropriate to the demonstrator's stage of development for this skill, needs to be a cue that will help develop this demonstrator's proficiency with the skill, and should be related to a feature clearly visible in the video.

You then might quickly fill out the main ideas you want to address in each part, like this:

Sample Notes—Ideas Under Each Main Part

1. Description of stage of development

   Select an acceptable framework for stages of development of motor skills.

   Indicate general characteristics that would be seen at that stage of development.

2. Description of two features seen in the video

   Descriptions for each of the two performers

   Features need to be those that are descriptive of the stage of development of the performer.

3. Verbal cue for one of the performers

Appropriate to stage of development

Help develop proficiency in the skill

Needs to be related to a feature of the skill performance clearly visible in the video.

You have now created the skeleton of your written response.

Writing Your Response

Now the important step of writing your response begins. The scorers will not consider your notes when they score your paper, so it is crucial that you integrate all the important ideas from your notes into your actual written response.

Some test takers believe that every written response on a Praxis test has to be in formal essay form, that is, with an introductory paragraph, then paragraphs with the response to the question, then a concluding paragraph. This is the case for very few Praxis tests (*English* and *Writing*). The *Movement Forms—Video Evaluation* test in physical education does not require formal essays, so you should use techniques that allow you to communicate information efficiently and clearly. For example, you can use bulleted or numbered lists or essay.

Returning to our sample question:

Let us assume that the visual stimulus from the video shows two children performing the fundamental locomotor skill of sliding. You observe that the first child appears to be doing the skill correctly. You would place the child in the Mature stage of development. You observe that the second child is having difficulty performing the skill correctly. You would place the child in the Initial stage of development.

See below how the outline of our response to the first part of the question can become the final written response in a list format:

Part 1

Demonstrator #1 appears to be in the Mature stage of development for this skill. The Mature stage of development for the locomotor skill of sliding includes the following features:

1. Moderate tempo
2. Smooth, rhythmical action
3. Trailing leg lands adjacent to or behind lead leg
4. Both legs flexed at 45-degree angles during flight
5. Low flight pattern

Demonstrator #2 appears to be in the Initial stage of development for this skill. The Initial stage of development for the locomotor skill of sliding includes the following features:

1. Trailing leg often fails to remain behind
2. Trailing leg often contacts surface in front of lead leg
3. Arms of little use in balance or force production
4. Rhythm not smooth

Prose format is also acceptable for any of the three parts of the question.

For example, you might choose to write the answer to Part 3 using prose. (Assume that for the second demonstrator you observed the child crossing his left leg in front of his right leg.)

Part 3

The key feature to work on with this child is the fact that he crosses his left leg over his right instead of closing the left to slightly behind his right (trailing leg often contacts surface in front of lead leg). I would cue the child to always have his right foot in front of the left (always lead with right foot). I might also have to work with the child about shifting his weight so that he could always lead with the right.

Whatever format you select, the important thing is that your answer needs to be thorough, complete, and detailed. You need to be certain that you are referring to the specific and relevant performances that are observed in the video.

Chapter 12

Practice Test, *Physical Education: Movement Forms—Video Evaluation*

▶   ▶   ▶   ▶   ▶   ▶   ▶   ▶   ▶   ▶   ▶   ▶

Now that you have worked through strategies and preparation relating to the *Physical Education: Movement Forms—Video Evaluation* test, you should take the following practice test. This test is an actual Praxis test, now retired. You will probably find it helpful to simulate actual testing conditions, giving yourself 60 minutes to work on the questions. You can use the lined answer pages provided if you wish.

When you are ready to start the test, start playing the DVD on a television or computer. The DVD will guide you through the administration—let it run, and it will present the demonstrators four times during the 60-minute testing time.

Keep in mind that the test you take at an actual administration will have different questions. You should not expect your level of performance to be exactly the same as when you take the test at an actual administration, since numerous factors affect a person's performance in any given testing situation.

When you have finished the practice questions, you can read through the sample responses with scorer annotations in chapter 13.

Professional Assessments for Beginning Teachers®

Educational Testing Service

TEST NAME:

Physical Education: Movement Forms—Video Evaluation (0093)

Time—60 Minutes

2 Questions

Begin playing the DVD and follow the directions.

Question 1

IN ANSWERING THE FOLLOWING, MAKE SPECIFIC REFERENCE TO THE PERFORMANCE OF THE FOUR DEMONSTRATORS IN THE VIDEO.

I. For <u>each</u> of the four demonstrators:

- Describe the stage of development in the skill that the demonstrator's performance indicates.
- Describe two important features of that stage of development that are clearly visible in the demonstrator's performance in the video.

II. For two of the demonstrators:

- Describe a verbal cue that you could give that demonstrator to help the demonstrator further develop proficiency in performing this skill. This cue should be appropriate to that demonstrator's stage of development in the skill and should be related to a feature of performance of the skill clearly visible in the video.

The four demonstrators shown in the video were instructed to dribble the basketball while walking from left to right, and then from right to left, in front of the camera; they were then instructed to dribble toward the camera from the end of the gymnasium. They were instructed to use the hand they felt most comfortable with throughout their demonstration.

NOTES

Question 2

IN ANSWERING THE FOLLOWING, MAKE SPECIFIC REFERENCE TO THE PERFORMANCE OF THE THREE DEMONSTRATORS IN THE VIDEO.

I   For <u>each</u> of the three demonstrators:

- Describe all incorrect features of that demonstrator's performance.
- Explain why each incorrect feature you identify for that demonstrator's performance reduces the effectiveness of the exercise as a test of muscular strength and endurance and/or as a means to improve muscular strength and endurance.

II.   For any demonstrator whose performance may result in harm to the body:

- Describe the features of that demonstrator's performance that make the way in which he or she is performing the exercise potentially harmful.
- Describe the nature of the physical injury that is likely to result from the way in which the demonstrator is performing the exercise.

You should use the recommendations concerning the performance of the sit-up contained in recent research and the most recent health-related fitness tests as a basis for judging the correctness and/or the potential harmfulness of the demonstrators' performances.

NOTES

Begin your response to Question 1 here.

(Question 1 continued)

(Question 1 continued)

_____

_____

_____

_____

_____

_____

_____

_____

_____

_____

_____

_____

_____

_____

_____

_____

_____

_____

_____

(Question 1 continued)

_____

_____

_____

_____

_____

_____

_____

_____

_____

_____

_____

_____

_____

_____

_____

_____

_____

_____

_____

_____

_____

(Question 1 continued)

_____

_____

_____

_____

_____

_____

_____

_____

_____

_____

_____

_____

_____

_____

_____

_____

_____

_____

_____

_____

Begin your response to Question 2 here.

_____

_____

_____

_____

_____

_____

_____

_____

_____

_____

_____

_____

_____

_____

_____

_____

_____

_____

_____

_____

_____

_____

(Question 2 continued)

(Question 2 continued)

(Question 2 continued)

(Question 2 continued)

_____

_____

_____

_____

_____

_____

_____

_____

_____

_____

_____

_____

_____

_____

_____

_____

_____

Chapter 13

Sample Responses and How They Were Scored, *Physical Education: Movement Forms—Video Evaluation*

▶ ▶ ▶ ▶ ▶ ▶ ▶ ▶ ▶ ▶ ▶ ▶

This chapter presents actual sample responses to the questions in the practice test and explanations for the scores they received.

As discussed in chapter 7, each question on the *Video Evaluation* test is scored on a scale from 0 to 6. The general scoring guide used to score these questions is reprinted here for your convenience.

Score	Comment
6	Demonstrates a superior understanding of the principles of physical education and their appropriate application
	Responds appropriately to all parts of the question
	Uses data provided in the question very accurately and effectively
	Provides very accurate, well-chosen, and well-developed descriptions of physical education activities
5	Demonstrates a strong understanding of the principles of physical education and their appropriate application
	Responds appropriately to all or nearly all parts of the question
	Uses data provided in the question accurately and effectively
	Provides accurate, well-chosen, and well-developed descriptions of physical education activities
4	Demonstrates an adequate understanding of the principles of physical education and their appropriate application
	Responds appropriately to at least most parts of the question
	Uses some data provided in the question fairly accurately and effectively
	Provides fairly accurate, well-chosen, and well-developed descriptions of physical education activities
3	Demonstrates some understanding of the principles of physical education and their appropriate application
	Responds appropriately to some parts of the question
	Uses data provided in the question, but may show some inaccuracy and/or vagueness in use of data
	Provides descriptions of physical education activities, but they may be somewhat deficient in relevance, accuracy, and/or development

2 Demonstrates limited understanding, and may show some misunderstanding, of the principles of physical education and their appropriate application

May respond appropriately to only a few parts of the question.

May use data provided in the question only in a very limited, inaccurate, and/or vague way

Provides descriptions of physical education activities, but they may be seriously deficient in relevance, accuracy, and/or development

1 Demonstrates little or no understanding, and may show serious misunderstanding, of the principles of physical education and their appropriate application

May fail to respond appropriately to any part of the question

May show serious inaccuracy and/or vagueness in use of data provided in the question, or may fail entirely to use such data

May fail to provide descriptions of physical education activities, or may provide descriptions that are seriously flawed in relevance, accuracy, and/or development

0 Blank, off-topic, or merely a restatement of the question

Question 1

We will now look at four actual responses to Question 1 and see how the scoring guide above was used to rate each response.

Sample 1: Score of 4 (out of a possible 5)

Four demonstrations on basketball dribble:

1st demonstrator:

This demonstrator used intense concentration during the dribble performance. The inconsistent nature of the dribble, the demonstrator even had to chase the ball down at some points in the demonstration.

I would identify this child to be at the <u>pre-control</u> stage of development.

2nd demo:

This demonstrator would be at the utilization level. I can not say that this demo would be at the proficiency level due to the walking patterns they were instructed to use for the camera. (there needs to be running & diagonal movement)

The important features for this demonstration would be the (1) controlled manner of the dribble and the (2) ability to use both hands during the demonstration. The demonstrator was able to look up during the dribble which signals a comfort level of this skill while maintaining control of the ball. The demonstrator's ability to use the cross-over dribble shows that this skill has been learned previously and there is a high comfort level with either hand for the dribble.

Demo 3:

This demonstrator could be identified at the pre-control level.

The demonstrator showed two features, inconsistency and the need for intense concentration, during the Performance. The demonstrator was inconsistent in the dribble pattern and rhythm and had to chase the ball at certain points of the demonstration. The demonstrator showed the need for intense concentration focusing only on the ball.

Demo 4:

Control stage of development. Student is fairly controlled with this movement but is still needing a lot concentration of the skill. The student is only comfortable with one hand.

1. Fairly Good Control
2. Still concentration on ball only

Verbal Cues:

Demo 1:

- use finger pads of hand
- use consistent rhythm of dribble
- start stationary—then movement when more comfortable
- bend knees more instead of back

Demo 2:

Dribble ball at waist level

Bend knees so not so up-right with movement

Practice looking up even more

Commentary on Sample 1:

Demonstrated some understanding of a framework for stages of development of the skill. Identified some features—needed to be more specific. Indicated cues for two demonstrators.

Sample 2: Score of 3 (out of a possible 5)

<u>Demonstrator A</u> → Initial stage of development × characteristics →

1. Eyes were constantly looking down at the ball. Only looked up to change directions.

2. Uses dominant hand only while dribbling

*Verbal cue → While dribbling use your finger tips when contacting the ball, not your palm.

<u>Demonstrator B</u> → Elementary stage of development. Second stage of development where students have more coordination and control of their bodies characteristics →

1. Attempted to use both hands.

2. Looks up while dribbling.

*Verbal cue → When you are dribbling keep the ball below your waist by bending your knees.

<u>Demonstrator C</u> → Initial stage of development. First stages of development where students lack control and coordination

Characteristics → 1. Limited extension at the elbow.

2. Unable to control the ball while dribbling.

<u>Demonstrator D</u> → Is in the initial stage of development

Characteristics of Stage → 1. Uses palm of hand to control ball instead of finger tips.

2. Only uses dominant hand while dribbling.

Commentary on Sample 2:

Demonstrated some misunderstanding of a framework for stages of development of the skill. Did identify mostly correct features for all of the demonstrators. Developed two cues. One would help develop proficiency for the indicated feature.

Sample 3: Score of 2 (out of a possible 5)

Dribbling a basketball for the children who were at the mature stage of development but a few of the children were not there yet.

A. intermediate
B. mature
C. intermediate
D. mature

Child B was mature because he dribbled with both hands and kept the ball close to him with his eyes ahead & had good ball control . Child C was not using correct arm motion to push the ball down so he had no control of the bounce. he was slapping at the ball.

For child C who was slapping at the ball I would have the child stand in one place & I would "push" the ball down. Then catch it at his belly. Then I would have him do it 10 times in a row so he can get the feeling of pushing the ball down. Then I would have him get with a partner & practice bounce passes so again he could feel what it is like to push the ball down instead of slapping at it.

For child D: who has pretty good ball control but never takes her eyes off the ball. I would let her know she has to look where she is dribbling so I would have her dribble around cones so she has to look ahead of her not just straight down. I would also let her know she is bouncing the ball a little to high. I would also have her start using the opposite hand

Commentary on Sample 3:

Demonstrated misunderstanding of a framework for stages of development of the skill. Identified some features correctly for two demonstrators. Developed one cue and discussed errors for a second demonstrator.

Sample 4: Score of 2 (out of a possible 5)

> Student A is in the cognitive stage. Student A has many errors in the skill. "A" is still learning about the skill verbally from the teacher. "A" repeats errors. I would use "fingers" for cue because "A" needs to use fingers instead of her palm to dibble ball.
>
> Student B is in the afferent stage. "B" is conscious of errors and has less errors in skill. I'd use "lower" to remind "B" to dribble ball lower so it is harder for opponent to steal.
>
> Student C is in the cognitive stage "C" is making many errors in the skill. "C" repeats errors. A verbal cue is "rhythm". "C" needs to bounce the ball to a rhythm or beat. "C" is consistently inconsistent with the dribble.
>
> Student D is in the afferent stage. "D" can make adjustments to errors but still makes little errors. Student "D" needs to bend the knee's when walking and dribbling. I would use "knees" as a verbal cue.

Commentary on Sample 4:

Demonstrated misunderstanding of a framework for stages of development of the skill. Identification of features of the performers was very limited. Description of cues was very limited.

Question 2

The scoring guide used for Question 1 is also applied to this question.

We will now look at four samples and see how the scoring guide was used to rate each part of the response.

Sample 5: Score of 5 (out of a possible 5)

> Student 2-A. Hand placement on neck, feet to far from hips, pulls on neck as she rises, left feel slightly comes to far forward.
>
> With sit-ups the only way to get effective intensity on the desired muscles of the abdomen area is with proper form. Because most of the force to raise the upper body in this position is thru the hip flexors, the abdominal muscle are not used to their fullest extent unless proper form is used. By pulling on here neck, she is among the load factors on her abs. With her feet so far from her hip she is placing most of

stress on the hip flexors not on the "Abs". When she raises or moves her feet her balance changes and the fulcrum point changes thus shifting the stress on the muscles being worked. The load for this student sit-up is on her hip flexors not her Abs.

Student 2-B. Her legs are straight—thus placing her body in an incorrect position. It also place the brunt of the stress on her lower back because she can not get the proper curl up position to focus the stress in her abs. She also moves her head—her chin raises off of her chest a potential chance for neck strain. She does demonstrate correct upper body position at the apex of her situp. Back straight shoulders and head lifted forward because the stress is on her low back and her hips can slide forward and back the effectiveness of this form to increase strength and the endurance is very low.

Student 2-C. Form is completely incorrect—lifts feet twists his trunk feet to far from body, head bounces, thrusts her body forward, keeps her back to straight and stiff. Because of all the incorrect form she is not focusing on the muscle in her "abs" but using any and all means to raise her body. At first glance her strength level is to lower to properly do the exercise. She needs to have the exercise broken down to fundamental parts to gain strength/endurance.

Student 2-13: improper leg position which puts to much strain on her low back. She can favor compression of her hips causing nerve damage, muscle strain, and hyper extension of her hips back and neck as she raises.

Commentary on Sample 5:

Identifies many incorrect features. Addressed why the indicated performance features would reduce the effectiveness of the exercise. Addressed one feature that made the exercise potentially harmful and discussed potential injury.

Sample 6: Score of 4 (out of a possible 5)

The three girls performing the sit-ups are all making some mistakes:

Girl A: Hands are behind the neck which can put strain on the neck and possibly injure it. It also reduces the effectiveness of the sit-ups as the abs muscles aren't being fairly used. She is also going chest to knees which is not necessary and does not continue to work the abs.

Girl B: Her hand position is good, but her leg position will cause lower back strain. She has them flat and tight. This causes her to have to pull with her lower back muscles instead of her abs. As she rises she is also extending, instead of tucking her chin. The fluid motion is good.

Girl C: This girl perhaps is more apt to hurt herself. Though her knees are beat, she is not keeping her feet on the floor. She is jerking to pull herself up, throwing her head forward, losing balance as she rises. She can cause injury to her neck and back by performing this way.

Girl B: Reduces the work in the ab. area by straightening her legs. She also increases the risk to lower back strain or injury. Locking the knees can also make knee strain as the body pulls up.

Girl C: She is using so many different parts of her body to pull herself up that she is not working the ab muscles effectively.

To perform sit-ups correctly, the goal should be to isolate the abs. With arms over chest and knees up, feet flat as the body moves up the pull is in the abdominal area. If the sit-up is being done incorrectly, it will take a longer time to develop the muscles and because of the possibility of injury can be counter-productive in building muscular strength and endurance.

Commentary on Sample 6:

Identified some incorrect features. Addressed why some of the performance features would reduce the effectiveness of the exercise. Addressed several performance features that made the exercise potentially harmful and indicated potential injury.

Sample 7: Score of 3 (out of a possible 5)

Part I

Example #1

Her form appear to be pretty good with the following exceptions. She is pulling on the back of her head to help raise her body to her knees. This will reduce her effectiveness by putting to much strain on her back & neck & reducing effect on her abdominals. Also, she tucks her chin down into her chest, thus reducing the effectiveness of her sit-ups & increasing stress on her neck and back. She "rolls" along her back on the way down.

Example #2

By extending her legs flat on the floor, she shifts the emphases of the exercise from her stomach (abdominals) to her lower back. At this point she is not able to develop her ab's. in the way she desires.

Example #3

To help her raise her body off the floor she is lifting her feet from the floor. This decrease her opportunity for an effective exercise. She uses the momentum created by lifting her feet, thus, she reduces the force put on her abs. Also, it switches the force from her abs to her lower back. Also, she jerks at the start of the sit-up. Bad for neck/back.

Part II

Demonstrator #2

She raises her upper body in a nice straight and erect posture; however, by keeping her legs extended flat on the floor she increases her chance for a lower back injury. She is forcing the muscles in her back to lift her instead of the muscles in her stomach. She could potentially develop a chronic lower back problem.

Commentary on Sample 7:

Identified some of the incorrect features. Attempted to address why the performance would reduce the effectiveness of the exercise. Addressed one feature that made the exercise potentially harmful and discussed potential injury.

Sample 8: Score of 2 (out of a possible 5)

Sit Ups

In response to demonstrators form. (Incorrect feature) Demonstrator A.

(1) Placed hands behind neck, this causes too much stress on neck.

(2) Even though legs are bent feet are flat on floor, demonstrator brings her upper torso too high. She can reduce strain and possible injury by lifting so her lower back comes off the floor just an inch. This is plenty of motion to work those abdominals.

Demonstrator B

(1) By not bending her legs she is creating an excessive strain on her lower back.

(2) She could also reduce needless lower back tension by reducing the length of her contraction

Demonstrator C

1) Arching her back prior to her sit up in order to gain momentum, is a good way to create a lower back injury.

2) Jerky movements, too fast. Slower, more controlled movements could help to develop the entire.

Commentary on Sample 8:

Identified some of the incorrect features. Identified some of the potential injuries. Did not address why performance would reduce the effectiveness of the exercise.

Chapter 14
Study Topics for the *Health Education* Test

▶   ▶   ▶   ▶   ▶   ▶   ▶   ▶   ▶   ▶   ▶   ▶

Introduction to the Test

The health education test is designed to assess the subject-area knowledge and competencies thought to be needed by a beginning teacher of health education. The topics covered in the test include the range of concepts studied in an undergraduate health education major program. However, some questions of a more advanced nature are included, because instructors must understand the subject matter from a more advanced viewpoint than that presented to their students. The questions will encompass theories and skills covered in courses in community, personal and social health; health promotion and disease prevention; nutrition and dietary patterns; sexuality and healthy relationships; physical fitness and wellness; and health-education-related pedagogy. Although the questions require a variety of abilities, they emphasize comprehension of critical concepts, use of analysis to address and solve problems, and an understanding of important terms. Some questions may require the examinee to integrate concepts from more than one content area.

Acquiring the knowledge, skills, and competencies necessary to teach health education will enable the teacher to plan, implement, manage, and evaluate the learning environment effectively. As a result of their understanding of the topics addressed in the health education test, teachers can develop effective curriculums, teaching strategies, and assessment practices.

The test is designed to reflect current standards for knowledge, skills, and abilities in health education. Educational Testing Service (ETS) has aligned this test closely with the National Health Education Standards and works in collaboration with teacher educators, higher education content specialists, and accomplished practicing teachers in the field of health education to keep the test updated and representative of current standards.

The content of the *Health Education* test includes 120 multiple-choice questions that are divided into the following categories:

- Health Education as a Discipline (15%)

- Promoting Healthy Lifestyles (30%)

- Community Health Advocacy (10%)

- Healthy Relationships (20%)

- Disease Prevention (15%)

- Health Education Pedagogy (10%)

While reviewing the study topics, be aware that a comprehensive health education program would cover the major characteristics of each topic. Your health education course of study should produce familiarity with many of the minor topics and some recognition of the subtopics included in the chapter. Consult materials and resources from all your health education course work. You should be able to match up specific topics and subtopics with what you have covered in your courses.

Try not to be overwhelmed by the volume and scope of content knowledge in this guide. An overview such as this, which lists health education topics, does not offer you a great deal of context. Although a specific term may not seem familiar as you see it here, you may find that you can understand it when it is applied to a real-life situation. Many of the items on the actual Praxis test will provide you with a context in which to apply to these topics or terms, as you will see when you look at the practice questions in chapter 15. Keep in mind that the subtopics and star questions below are used for study purposes only and don't include everything that could be on the test.

Special questions marked with stars:

Interspersed throughout the list of topics are questions that are outlined in boxes and preceded by stars (★). These questions are intended to help you test your knowledge of fundamental concepts and your ability to apply the concepts to situations in the real world. Most of the questions require you to combine several pieces of knowledge in order to formulate an integrated understanding and response. If you spend time on these questions, you will gain increased understanding and facility with the subject matter covered on the test. You might want to discuss these questions and your answers with a teacher or mentor.

Note that the questions marked with stars are not short-answer or multiple-choice and that this study guide does not provide the answers. The questions marked with stars are intended as study questions, not practice questions. Thinking about the answers to them should improve your understanding of fundamental concepts and will probably help you answer a broad range of questions on the test.

CONTENT DESCRIPTION

Health Education as a Discipline

A. Health literacy: the set of skills and knowledge required to read, understand, and act on basic health information and services. It can be affected by difficulties with basic literacy, age, cultural differences, or second-language learning.

- Critical thinking and problem solving

- Effective communication

- Responsible and productive citizenship

- Self-directed learning

★ **Explain the four characteristics identified as essential for the health-literate person.**

B. Responsibilities and competencies for entry-level health educators: the set of skills and expectations one should possess when beginning a career as a health educator.

- Assessing individual and community needs for health education

- Planning effective health education programs

- Implementing health education programs

- Evaluating the effectiveness of health education programs

- Coordinating the provision of health education services

- Acting as a resource person in health education

- Communicating health and health education needs, concerns, and resources.

★ **For each responsibility above, give an example of a related activity that is appropriate for a school setting.**

C. National Health Education Standards: the standards that detail what students should know and be able to do in health education. As a result of study in health education, students will

- Comprehend concepts related to health promotion and disease prevention

- Demonstrate the ability to access valid health information and health-related products and services

- Demonstrate the ability to practice health-enhancing behaviors and reduce health risks

- Analyze the influence of culture, media, technology, and other factors on health

- Demonstrate the ability to use interpersonal communication skills to enhance health

- Demonstrate the ability to use goal-setting and decision-making skills to enhance health

- Demonstrate the ability to advocate for personal, family, and community health

★ **Explain the two types of knowledge included within the National Health Education Standards.**

D. Morbidity, mortality, and behavioral risk data: data that show the leading causes of death and illness.

- Youth Risk Behavior Surveillance System (YRBSS)

- Behavioral Risk Factor Surveillance Survey (BRFSS)

- School Health Policies and Programs Study (SHPPS)

- Morbidity and Mortality Weekly Report (MMWR)

★ **What health-related behaviors are identified in the YRBSS as those that contribute most markedly to premature death?**

E. Adolescent risk behaviors identified by the Centers for Disease Control and Prevention: six types of behavior during adolescence that cause the most serious problems that impact the United States population. These behaviors usually are established during youth, persist into adulthood, are interrelated, and are preventable. In addition to causing serious health problems, these behaviors contribute to many of the educational and social problems that confront the nation, including failure to complete high school, unemployment, and crime.

- Unintentional/intentional injuries

- HIV, sexually transmitted infections (STIs), unintended pregnancy

- Tobacco

- Alcohol and other drugs

- Dietary patterns

- Sedentary lifestyles

★ **According to research on adolescent risk behaviors, what are some of the family-related factors that contribute to these problem behaviors among youth?**

F. Health behavior theories: theories that provide frameworks for examining health behavior change and for designing targeted interventions. For example, the health belief model; the transtheoretical model and stages of change; the theory of reasoned action; the theory of planned behavior; health locus of control; transactional model of stress and coping; social-cognitive theory; social networks and social support; community organization; diffusion of innovations; communication theory; organizational change; ecological models; attribution theory; cognitive consistency theory, etc.

★ **Explain the difference between interpersonal (behaviorist) and intrapersonal (humanist) theories in health education, and provide an example of each.**

G. Coordinated school health: a school health approach designed to help young people grow into healthy and productive adults by focusing on the physical, emotional, intellectual, and social well-being of children in kindergarten through twelfth grade. It strives to provide students with the information and skills they will need to make good choices in life. An effective school health plan works in partnership with parents/caregivers, health personnel, community-based agencies, and others. The program recognizes that health and learning go hand in hand to facilitate students' achievement and success. The eight components of coordinated school health include

- Health education

- Physical education

- Health services

- Nutrition services

- Health promotion for staff

- Counseling, psychological, and social services

- Healthy school environment

- Family/community involvement

★ **What is the role of physical education in a coordinated school health program?**

H. Health/Wellness domains: the definitions of the interrelated domains of health and wellness. The dimensions of wellness go beyond the absence of disease and incorporate multifaceted behaviors that improve health and the quality of life. The domains include physical, social, mental, emotional, spiritual, environmental, occupational health, etc.

★ **Describe the concept of spiritual health and explain how this may be different from or similar to one's religious beliefs.**

I. Science foundations related to health: biology, chemistry, physiology, psychology, epidemiology, sociology, etc.

★ **Define the foundational science of epidemiology as it relates to health education.**

J. Code of Ethics for the Health Education Profession: the document that describes how the health education profession is dedicated to excellence in the practice of promoting individual, family, organizational, and community health. The Code of Ethics provides a framework of shared values within which health education is practiced. The responsibility of all health educators is to aspire to the highest possible standards of conduct and to encourage the ethical behavior of all those with whom they work.

- Article I: Responsibility to the Public

- Article II: Responsibility to the Profession

- Article III: Responsibility to Employers

- Article IV: Responsibility in the Delivery of Health Education

- Article V: Responsibility in Research and Evaluation

- Article VI: Responsibility in Professional Preparation

> ★ **What are the five basic principles of human morality that are usually applied to the field of health education ethics?**
>
> ★ **On what fundamental ethical principles is the Code of Ethics based?**

Promoting Healthy Lifestyles

A. Individual responsibility for healthy lifestyles

- Goal setting

- Decision making

> ★ **Describe the steps that an individual might use when developing a goal to change a health-related behavior.**

B. The components of physical fitness: health-related fitness (aerobic endurance, muscular strength and endurance, muscular flexibility, and body composition), and skill-related fitness (agility, balance, coordination, power, reaction time, and speed).

- Body composition

- Cardiorespiratory endurance (cardiovascular fitness)

- Flexibility

- Muscular strength and endurance

- Individualizing exercise programs

- Frequency

- Duration

- Mode

- Intensity

> ★ **Define body composition and explain two methods that can be used to assess an individual's body composition.**

C. Nutrition: how the diet should supply essential nutrients required for proper body growth, maintenance, and repair, plus the energy necessary for daily activities including work, play, and rest.

- Basic food groups/dietary goals (USDA Food Guide Pyramids)

- Nutrients, metabolism, calories, and fad diets

- Dietary guidelines for Americans

- Dietary patterns

- Nutritional facts (food labels)

> ★ **Describe the function of carbohydrates in the body and differentiate between simple and complex carbohydrates.**

D. Stress management and coping skills: healthy and unhealthy responses. Stress is the body's response to life's situations. It can be positive or negative, but it is impossible to live without some degree of stress. A healthy response requires adaptation to the stress we experience.

- The physiological response to stress; general adaptation syndrome

- The physiological response to relaxation, and relaxation techniques (biofeedback, massage, meditation, hypnosis, etc.)

- The role of personality and social support

★ **Explain the difference between stress, distress, and eustress.**

E. Reducing and preventing health risks: how most of the health risks that we face in our lives are a result of the behaviors we practice. Proper attention to healthier behaviors will help reduce and prevent illness.

- Unintentional/intentional injuries (personal safety, basic first-aid techniques)

- HIV, STIs, unintended pregnancy

- Tobacco

- Alcohol and other drugs (over-the-counter drugs, prescription drugs, generic drugs, illegal substances, "non-drug drugs" [e.g., caffeine], causes for the use and abuse of substances, alternate coping skills, physical and psychological effects, treatment)

- Dietary patterns

- Sedentary lifestyles

★ **What are the major health risks/behaviors associated with the development of coronary heart disease?**

F. Anatomy and physiology (body systems)

- Nervous system

- Endocrine system

- Cardiovascular system

- Respiratory system

- Digestive system

- Renal system

- Reproductive system

- Immune system

- Skeletal system

- Muscular system

★ **Describe the function of the immune system and explain which internal organs help regulate and control the immunity of a healthy individual.**

Community Health Advocacy

A. Health and safety laws and regulations

- Disease reporting

- Confidentiality

- Work/Recreational safety

- Controlled substances

- Immunizations

- Tobacco use

- Disabilities

> ★ **Explain the function of the Occupational Safety and Health Administration (OSHA), the American Conference of Governmental Industrial Hygienists (ACGIH), the Environmental Protection Agency (EPA), and the National Institute for Occupational Safety and Health (NIOSH) in regulating limits for exposure to hazardous products within the workplace.**

B. Environmental health issues

- Waste (e.g., solid and hazardous)

- Pollution (e.g., air, water, noise)

- Chemical hazards (e.g., pesticides)

- Biological hazards (e.g., infectious diseases)

> ★ **Discuss the concepts of bioconcentration (bioamplification).**
>
> ★ **Describe the Ambient Air Quality Standard.**

C. Consumer health (quackery, advertising, health care delivery systems, insurance, importance of regular checkups, personal responsibility for health care, health myths)

> ★ **What criteria can consumers use to distinguish between accurate and fraudulent health product claims?**

D. Access to valid health information, products, and services

> ★ **How can an individual evaluate the validity of health information from the Internet?**

E. Health careers (types of occupational positions, career possibilities, educational requirements prior to training, formal training required [number of years, types of programs])

> ★ **Describe the differences between allopathic, osteopathic, ayurvedic, and chiropractic medicine.**

F. Health agencies (public vs. private, services provided, cost considerations, health-care delivery systems)

★ **What are the primary purposes of voluntary health agencies?**

★ **Explain the difference between a health maintenance organization and a fee-for-service type of health care delivery.**

G. Leadership

★ **What are the leadership skills necessary for directing groups through a decision-making process within a health education setting?**

H. Community service

★ **Describe the concept of service learning, and explain how it can be applied to the enlistment of volunteers to serve in the community.**

Healthy Relationships

A. Decision-making skills

★ **What are the steps involved in the decision-making process?**

B. Growth and development

- Life stages

- Death and dying

★ **What are the stages of grief described by Kübler-Ross?**

C. Psychosocial development: a complex interaction of the emotional, mental, social, and spiritual dimensions of health that contribute to our perceptions of self and others.

- Family-structure relationships

- Peer relationships

- Self-concept

- Self-esteem

- Character education

★ **Describe the differences between the commonly interchanged terms of self-concept, self-esteem, and self-efficacy.**

D. Interpersonal communication

- Conflict resolution

- Assertiveness

- Refusal skills

- "I" messages

- Active listening

★ **Explain the differences between aggressive, assertive, and passive behaviors.**

E. Dating, marriage/partnerships, and parenting

- Readiness and responsibility

★ **Describe the roles of commitment and emotional intimacy in a relationship.**

F. Sexuality: how understanding sexual behavior and learning to make responsible choices can lead to a healthier and richer life.

- Reproductive choices

- Sexual expression

- Sexual difficulties

- Pregnancy and infertility

★ **What factors are generally considered when determining one's sexual identity?**

G. Violence: behaviors that produce physical and psychological injury, whether intentional or unintentional.

- Abuse (physical, verbal, emotional, and sexual)

- Bullying and harassment

- Terrorism

★ **Describe the cultural, individual, and social factors that have been shown to increase the likelihood that someone will commit a violent act.**

H. Diverse populations: meeting a pluralistic society's needs for health education relative to differing socioeconomic, cultural, and ethnic backgrounds

★ **What are the dimensions of diversity that should be considered in health education?**

Disease Prevention

A. Health conditions

- Acute and chronic

- Communicable and noncommunicable

- Infectious and noninfectious

- Genetic

- Congenital

- Environment related

- Myths and misconceptions

- Pain and pain management

★ **What are the most common modes of disease transmission?**

B. Mental and emotional health, including our thoughts and feelings related to an individual's values, attitudes, and beliefs. Many internal and external factors such as family support or self-esteem influence a person's mental and emotional health.

- Depression

- Suicide

- Addictive behaviors

- Eating disorders

- Classification of mental illness

- Defense mechanisms

★ **Describe the symptoms commonly associated with depression.**

C. Treatment and counseling

- Therapy and psychotherapy

★ **Explain the differences between psychodynamic and cognitive-behavior forms of therapy.**

D. Hygiene: practicing behaviors that help promote health through eliminating unsanitary conditions.

★ **What simple hygienic strategy is most commonly recommended to avoid overexposure to harmful pathogens?**

Health Education Pedagogy

A. Assessing needs (individual and community)

★ **Describe how you would use the "recede-proceed" model in developing a health education program in a K-12 school environment.**

B. Planning (performance-based objectives, curriculum, and programs)

★ **Explain the concepts of scope and sequence within a health education curriculum.**

C. Implementing (methods, strategies, and techniques)

★ **Discuss the differences between direct and indirect styles of teaching within a health education curriculum.**

D. Evaluating (student learning and teacher effectiveness)

★ **Describe the differences between formative and summative forms of evaluation.**

★ **Explain what a rubric is and how you would construct one.**

Chapter 15
Practice Test, *Health Education*

▶ ▶ ▶ ▶ ▶ ▶ ▶ ▶ ▶ ▶ ▶ ▶

Now that you have studied the content topics and have worked through strategies relating to multiple-choice questions, you should take the following practice test. You will probably find it helpful to give yourself about 75 minutes to work on the questions, so you will have approximately the same amount of time per question as you would encounter under real testing conditions. You can cut out and use the answer sheet provided if you wish.

Keep in mind that the test you take at an actual administration will have different questions, and a total of 120 questions, although the proportion of questions in each area and major subarea will be approximately the same. You should not expect the percentage of questions you answer correctly in these practice questions to be exactly the same as when you take the test at an actual administration, since numerous factors affect a person's performance in any given testing situation.

When you have finished the practice questions, you can score your answers and read the explanations of the best answer choices in chapter 16.

Educational
Testing Service

TEST NAME:

Health Education:
Practice Questions (0550)

Time—75 Minutes

75 Questions

(Note: At the official administration of test 0550, there will be 120 multiple-choice questions, and you will be allowed 120 minutes to complete the test.)

DO NOT USE INK

Use only a pencil with soft black lead (No. 2 or HB) to complete this answer sheet.
Be sure to fill in completely the oval that corresponds to the proper letter or number.
Completely erase any errors or stray marks.

Answer Sheet C

PAGE 1

THE PRAXIS SERIES®
Professional Assessments for Beginning Teachers®

1. NAME

Enter your last name and first initial.
Omit spaces, hyphens, apostrophes, etc.

Last Name (first 6 letters) | F I

2.

YOUR NAME: _____ _____ _____
(Print) Last Name (Family or Surname) First Name (Given) M. I.

MAILING ADDRESS: _____ _____
(Print) P.O. Box or Street Address Apt. # (if any)

_____ _____
City State or Province

_____ _____
Country Zip or Postal Code

TELEPHONE NUMBER: ( ) _____ ( ) _____
Home Business

SIGNATURE: _____ **TEST DATE:** _____

3. DATE OF BIRTH

| Month | Day |

Jan.
Feb.
Mar.
April
May
June
July
Aug.
Sept.
Oct.
Nov.
Dec.

4. SOCIAL SECURITY NUMBER

5. CANDIDATE ID NUMBER

6. TEST CENTER / REPORTING LOCATION

_____ _____
Center Number Room Number

_____
Center Name

_____ _____
City State or Province

_____
Country

7. TEST CODE / FORM CODE

8. TEST BOOK SERIAL NUMBER

9. TEST FORM

10. TEST NAME

Educational Testing Service, ETS, the ETS logo, and THE PRAXIS SERIES:PROFESSIONAL
ASSESSMENTS FOR BEGINNING TEACHERS and its logo are registered trademarks of
Educational Testing Service.

ETS Educational Testing Service

51055 • 08920 • TF71M500
MH01159   Q2573-06

I.N. 202974

1 2 3 4

CERTIFICATION STATEMENT: (Please write the following statement below. DO NOT PRINT.)
"I hereby agree to the conditions set forth in the *Registration Bulletin* and certify that I am the person whose name and address appear on this answer sheet."

_____

_____

_____

SIGNATURE: _____ DATE: _____ / _____ / _____

Month   Day   Year

BE SURE EACH MARK IS DARK AND COMPLETELY FILLS THE INTENDED SPACE AS ILLUSTRATED HERE: ● .

1 Ⓐ Ⓑ Ⓒ Ⓓ	41 Ⓐ Ⓑ Ⓒ Ⓓ	81 Ⓐ Ⓑ Ⓒ Ⓓ	121 Ⓐ Ⓑ Ⓒ Ⓓ
2 Ⓐ Ⓑ Ⓒ Ⓓ	42 Ⓐ Ⓑ Ⓒ Ⓓ	82 Ⓐ Ⓑ Ⓒ Ⓓ	122 Ⓐ Ⓑ Ⓒ Ⓓ
3 Ⓐ Ⓑ Ⓒ Ⓓ	43 Ⓐ Ⓑ Ⓒ Ⓓ	83 Ⓐ Ⓑ Ⓒ Ⓓ	123 Ⓐ Ⓑ Ⓒ Ⓓ
4 Ⓐ Ⓑ Ⓒ Ⓓ	44 Ⓐ Ⓑ Ⓒ Ⓓ	84 Ⓐ Ⓑ Ⓒ Ⓓ	124 Ⓐ Ⓑ Ⓒ Ⓓ
5 Ⓐ Ⓑ Ⓒ Ⓓ	45 Ⓐ Ⓑ Ⓒ Ⓓ	85 Ⓐ Ⓑ Ⓒ Ⓓ	125 Ⓐ Ⓑ Ⓒ Ⓓ
6 Ⓐ Ⓑ Ⓒ Ⓓ	46 Ⓐ Ⓑ Ⓒ Ⓓ	86 Ⓐ Ⓑ Ⓒ Ⓓ	126 Ⓐ Ⓑ Ⓒ Ⓓ
7 Ⓐ Ⓑ Ⓒ Ⓓ	47 Ⓐ Ⓑ Ⓒ Ⓓ	87 Ⓐ Ⓑ Ⓒ Ⓓ	127 Ⓐ Ⓑ Ⓒ Ⓓ
8 Ⓐ Ⓑ Ⓒ Ⓓ	48 Ⓐ Ⓑ Ⓒ Ⓓ	88 Ⓐ Ⓑ Ⓒ Ⓓ	128 Ⓐ Ⓑ Ⓒ Ⓓ
9 Ⓐ Ⓑ Ⓒ Ⓓ	49 Ⓐ Ⓑ Ⓒ Ⓓ	89 Ⓐ Ⓑ Ⓒ Ⓓ	129 Ⓐ Ⓑ Ⓒ Ⓓ
10 Ⓐ Ⓑ Ⓒ Ⓓ	50 Ⓐ Ⓑ Ⓒ Ⓓ	90 Ⓐ Ⓑ Ⓒ Ⓓ	130 Ⓐ Ⓑ Ⓒ Ⓓ
11 Ⓐ Ⓑ Ⓒ Ⓓ	51 Ⓐ Ⓑ Ⓒ Ⓓ	91 Ⓐ Ⓑ Ⓒ Ⓓ	131 Ⓐ Ⓑ Ⓒ Ⓓ
12 Ⓐ Ⓑ Ⓒ Ⓓ	52 Ⓐ Ⓑ Ⓒ Ⓓ	92 Ⓐ Ⓑ Ⓒ Ⓓ	132 Ⓐ Ⓑ Ⓒ Ⓓ
13 Ⓐ Ⓑ Ⓒ Ⓓ	53 Ⓐ Ⓑ Ⓒ Ⓓ	93 Ⓐ Ⓑ Ⓒ Ⓓ	133 Ⓐ Ⓑ Ⓒ Ⓓ
14 Ⓐ Ⓑ Ⓒ Ⓓ	54 Ⓐ Ⓑ Ⓒ Ⓓ	94 Ⓐ Ⓑ Ⓒ Ⓓ	134 Ⓐ Ⓑ Ⓒ Ⓓ
15 Ⓐ Ⓑ Ⓒ Ⓓ	55 Ⓐ Ⓑ Ⓒ Ⓓ	95 Ⓐ Ⓑ Ⓒ Ⓓ	135 Ⓐ Ⓑ Ⓒ Ⓓ
16 Ⓐ Ⓑ Ⓒ Ⓓ	56 Ⓐ Ⓑ Ⓒ Ⓓ	96 Ⓐ Ⓑ Ⓒ Ⓓ	136 Ⓐ Ⓑ Ⓒ Ⓓ
17 Ⓐ Ⓑ Ⓒ Ⓓ	57 Ⓐ Ⓑ Ⓒ Ⓓ	97 Ⓐ Ⓑ Ⓒ Ⓓ	137 Ⓐ Ⓑ Ⓒ Ⓓ
18 Ⓐ Ⓑ Ⓒ Ⓓ	58 Ⓐ Ⓑ Ⓒ Ⓓ	98 Ⓐ Ⓑ Ⓒ Ⓓ	138 Ⓐ Ⓑ Ⓒ Ⓓ
19 Ⓐ Ⓑ Ⓒ Ⓓ	59 Ⓐ Ⓑ Ⓒ Ⓓ	99 Ⓐ Ⓑ Ⓒ Ⓓ	139 Ⓐ Ⓑ Ⓒ Ⓓ
20 Ⓐ Ⓑ Ⓒ Ⓓ	60 Ⓐ Ⓑ Ⓒ Ⓓ	100 Ⓐ Ⓑ Ⓒ Ⓓ	140 Ⓐ Ⓑ Ⓒ Ⓓ
21 Ⓐ Ⓑ Ⓒ Ⓓ	61 Ⓐ Ⓑ Ⓒ Ⓓ	101 Ⓐ Ⓑ Ⓒ Ⓓ	141 Ⓐ Ⓑ Ⓒ Ⓓ
22 Ⓐ Ⓑ Ⓒ Ⓓ	62 Ⓐ Ⓑ Ⓒ Ⓓ	102 Ⓐ Ⓑ Ⓒ Ⓓ	142 Ⓐ Ⓑ Ⓒ Ⓓ
23 Ⓐ Ⓑ Ⓒ Ⓓ	63 Ⓐ Ⓑ Ⓒ Ⓓ	103 Ⓐ Ⓑ Ⓒ Ⓓ	143 Ⓐ Ⓑ Ⓒ Ⓓ
24 Ⓐ Ⓑ Ⓒ Ⓓ	64 Ⓐ Ⓑ Ⓒ Ⓓ	104 Ⓐ Ⓑ Ⓒ Ⓓ	144 Ⓐ Ⓑ Ⓒ Ⓓ
25 Ⓐ Ⓑ Ⓒ Ⓓ	65 Ⓐ Ⓑ Ⓒ Ⓓ	105 Ⓐ Ⓑ Ⓒ Ⓓ	145 Ⓐ Ⓑ Ⓒ Ⓓ
26 Ⓐ Ⓑ Ⓒ Ⓓ	66 Ⓐ Ⓑ Ⓒ Ⓓ	106 Ⓐ Ⓑ Ⓒ Ⓓ	146 Ⓐ Ⓑ Ⓒ Ⓓ
27 Ⓐ Ⓑ Ⓒ Ⓓ	67 Ⓐ Ⓑ Ⓒ Ⓓ	107 Ⓐ Ⓑ Ⓒ Ⓓ	147 Ⓐ Ⓑ Ⓒ Ⓓ
28 Ⓐ Ⓑ Ⓒ Ⓓ	68 Ⓐ Ⓑ Ⓒ Ⓓ	108 Ⓐ Ⓑ Ⓒ Ⓓ	148 Ⓐ Ⓑ Ⓒ Ⓓ
29 Ⓐ Ⓑ Ⓒ Ⓓ	69 Ⓐ Ⓑ Ⓒ Ⓓ	109 Ⓐ Ⓑ Ⓒ Ⓓ	149 Ⓐ Ⓑ Ⓒ Ⓓ
30 Ⓐ Ⓑ Ⓒ Ⓓ	70 Ⓐ Ⓑ Ⓒ Ⓓ	110 Ⓐ Ⓑ Ⓒ Ⓓ	150 Ⓐ Ⓑ Ⓒ Ⓓ
31 Ⓐ Ⓑ Ⓒ Ⓓ	71 Ⓐ Ⓑ Ⓒ Ⓓ	111 Ⓐ Ⓑ Ⓒ Ⓓ	151 Ⓐ Ⓑ Ⓒ Ⓓ
32 Ⓐ Ⓑ Ⓒ Ⓓ	72 Ⓐ Ⓑ Ⓒ Ⓓ	112 Ⓐ Ⓑ Ⓒ Ⓓ	152 Ⓐ Ⓑ Ⓒ Ⓓ
33 Ⓐ Ⓑ Ⓒ Ⓓ	73 Ⓐ Ⓑ Ⓒ Ⓓ	113 Ⓐ Ⓑ Ⓒ Ⓓ	153 Ⓐ Ⓑ Ⓒ Ⓓ
34 Ⓐ Ⓑ Ⓒ Ⓓ	74 Ⓐ Ⓑ Ⓒ Ⓓ	114 Ⓐ Ⓑ Ⓒ Ⓓ	154 Ⓐ Ⓑ Ⓒ Ⓓ
35 Ⓐ Ⓑ Ⓒ Ⓓ	75 Ⓐ Ⓑ Ⓒ Ⓓ	115 Ⓐ Ⓑ Ⓒ Ⓓ	155 Ⓐ Ⓑ Ⓒ Ⓓ
36 Ⓐ Ⓑ Ⓒ Ⓓ	76 Ⓐ Ⓑ Ⓒ Ⓓ	116 Ⓐ Ⓑ Ⓒ Ⓓ	156 Ⓐ Ⓑ Ⓒ Ⓓ
37 Ⓐ Ⓑ Ⓒ Ⓓ	77 Ⓐ Ⓑ Ⓒ Ⓓ	117 Ⓐ Ⓑ Ⓒ Ⓓ	157 Ⓐ Ⓑ Ⓒ Ⓓ
38 Ⓐ Ⓑ Ⓒ Ⓓ	78 Ⓐ Ⓑ Ⓒ Ⓓ	118 Ⓐ Ⓑ Ⓒ Ⓓ	158 Ⓐ Ⓑ Ⓒ Ⓓ
39 Ⓐ Ⓑ Ⓒ Ⓓ	79 Ⓐ Ⓑ Ⓒ Ⓓ	119 Ⓐ Ⓑ Ⓒ Ⓓ	159 Ⓐ Ⓑ Ⓒ Ⓓ
40 Ⓐ Ⓑ Ⓒ Ⓓ	80 Ⓐ Ⓑ Ⓒ Ⓓ	120 Ⓐ Ⓑ Ⓒ Ⓓ	160 Ⓐ Ⓑ Ⓒ Ⓓ

FOR ETS USE ONLY	R1	R2	R3	R4	R5	R6	R7	R8	TR	CS

HEALTH EDUCATION

Knowledge → Attitudes → Values → Health behavior

1. In the diagram above of a common health education concept, which of the following best characterizes "knowledge"?

   (A) Appropriate health knowledge has little value in forming positive health behavior.
   (B) The value of health knowledge as a single factor affecting positive health behavior is questionable.
   (C) Attitudes can be formed in a vacuum, without any prior knowledge.
   (D) Knowledge cannot influence attitudes, either positively or negatively.

2. Epidemiological assessment in health education calls for planning that is based on determining which of the following for a given target population?

   (A) Which medical technologies make life easier and equally comfortable for all members of the population
   (B) What health problems, measured objectively, pose the greatest threat to quality of life for the population
   (C) Which ecological factors contribute to the survival of the fittest in the population
   (D) What health standards are in place and what the health status of the population is

3. The study of the distribution and dynamics of disease is known as

   (A) morbidity
   (B) epidemiology
   (C) pathology
   (D) ecology

4. Which of the following statements best describes a coordinated school health program?

   (A) The aggregate of all purposeful activities designed to improve personal and public health
   (B) An organized set of policies, procedures, and activities designed to protect and promote the health and well-being of students and staff
   (C) The combination of educational and environmental supports for actions and conditions of living conducive to health
   (D) A partnership of both private and public efforts of individuals, groups, and organizations to promote, protect, and preserve the health of those in the community

5. The Centers for Disease Control and Prevention (CDC) maintains a national database of behavioral data for adolescents that can assist health educators in planning programs. The title of the database is

   (A) *Healthy People 2010*
   (B) The Youth Risk Behavior Surveillance System
   (C) *Morbidity and Mortality Weekly Report*
   (D) The Adolescent Risk Profile

6. Which of the following best represents the relationship of mortality to morbidity?

	Mortality	Morbidity
(A)	Death rate	Illness rate
(B)	Death rate	Injury rate
(C)	Illness rate	Death rate
(D)	Injury rate	Illness rate

7. Which of the following behaviors is LEAST likely to be characteristic of a health-literate person?

(A) Gathering current, reliable health information from a variety of sources before deciding on a dieting program

(B) Working collaboratively with community members to promote smokers' rights

(C) Advocating for daily physical education in local schools

(D) Implementing conflict-management skills to resolve a family dispute

8. Which of the following is NOT a major responsibility for entry-level health educators?

(A) Assessing individual and community needs for health education

(B) Implementing health education programs in schools

(C) Evaluating the effectiveness of health education programs

(D) Advocating for more funding for health education programs

9. Two types of knowledge are included in the National Health Education Standards. The first type is knowledge of health content. The second type is knowledge of

(A) process and skills as applied to healthy living

(B) benchmarks and performance standards

(C) how policy makers affect health education

(D) the rationale behind the standards

10. Which of the following behaviors contributes most to teenagers' mortality and morbidity?

(A) Alcohol and other drug use, sexual behaviors, and behaviors that result in injury

(B) Sexual behaviors, school truancy, and tobacco use

(C) School truancy, misuse of contraception, alcohol, and other drugs

(D) Behaviors that result in injury, falls, and sexual behaviors

11. The primary purpose of physical education within a coordinated school health program is to

(A) emphasize physical fitness activities only

(B) provide a planned and sequential instruction program promoting lifelong activity

(C) provide a basic-skills program that serves as a prerequisite to competitive sport

(D) focus on physical development and nutrition education

12. Which of the following fundamental ethical principles is NOT included in the Code of Ethics for the Health Education Profession?

   (A) Respect for autonomy
   (B) Promotion of social justice
   (C) Loyalty of decision makers
   (D) Avoidance of harm

13. Which of the following activities is most suitable for an aerobics program designed to develop cardiovascular endurance?

   (A) Weight lifting
   (B) Isometrics
   (C) Jogging
   (D) Gymnastics

14. Adolescent behavioral risk factors associated with families and that impact adolescent problem behaviors include all of the following EXCEPT

   (A) family conflicts
   (B) family management problems
   (C) family support services
   (D) parental attitudes favorable toward the problem behavior

15. The first evidence that an individual is being affected by alcohol is an impairment of

   (A) judgment and inhibitions
   (B) visual acuity
   (C) motor coordination
   (D) regularity in the breathing rate

16. Which of the following means of contraception is considered the best protection against sexually transmitted infections?

   (A) The use of a vaginal sponge
   (B) The use of vaginal spermicides
   (C) Sterilization
   (D) The use of a condom

17. The *Dietary Guidelines for Americans* recommends that most of the calories in the diet come from which of the following sources?

   (A) Saturated fats
   (B) Unsaturated fats
   (C) Carbohydrates
   (D) Proteins

18. The number of calories in a single serving of product X is 120. Product X includes a total of 6 grams of fat. For a single serving, which of the following correctly reflects the number of calories that come from fat and the percent of the serving that is made up of fat?

	Calories from Fat	Percent of Fat
(A)	24	20%
(B)	40	33%
(C)	54	45%
(D)	60	50%

19. Which of the following describes the correct procedures in emergency care, in order of highest to lowest priority?

(A) Rescue from an immediately dangerous situation, control severe bleeding, care for fractures, care for stoppage of breathing.

(B) Care for stoppage of breathing, control severe bleeding, care for fractures, rescue from an immediately dangerous situation.

(C) Control severe bleeding, care for stoppage of breathing, care for fractures, rescue from an immediately dangerous situation.

(D) Rescue from an immediately dangerous situation, care for the stoppage of breathing, control severe bleeding, care for fractures.

20. The shift in major causes of morbidity and mortality from infectious to chronic disease has presented health educators with the challenge of

(A) finding ways to promote personal behavior changes and a healthy lifestyle

(B) increasing medical services provided by advanced technology

(C) increasing government spending on health care

(D) eliminating risk-taking behavior

21. Which of the following sexually transmitted infections results in chronic illness even when treated medically?

(A) Syphilis

(B) Genital herpes

(C) Chlamydia

(D) Vaginitis

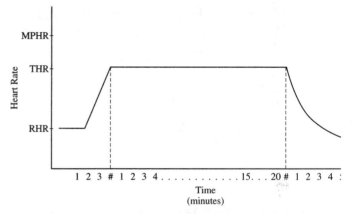

MPHR = Maximum performance heart rate
THR = Target heart rate
RHR = Resting heart rate

22. The graph above suggests that the participant has engaged in

(A) a strength-training program

(B) cardiovascular endurance workout

(C) a flexing and stretching activity

(D) an anaerobic conditioning session

23. An individual takes in 2,350 calories a day, but uses only 2,000 calories. In 30 days that individual can be expected to have gained approximately

(A) 2 pounds

(B) 3 pounds

(C) 4 pounds

(D) 5 pounds

24. Which of the following drugs is generally considered a depressant?

(A) Cocaine

(B) Lysergic acid diethylamide (LSD)

(C) Alcohol

(D) Methamphetamine

25. Which of the following describes the correct sequence of procedures when cardiopulmonary resuscitation (CPR) is performed after unresponsiveness has been established?

    (A) Open airway, ventilate twice, begin chest compressions, determine breathlessness and pulselessness after one minute.

    (B) Open airway, determine breathlessness, ventilate twice, determine pulselessness, begin chest compressions.

    (C) Open airway, ventilate twice, determine breathlessness, determine pulselessness, begin chest compressions.

    (D) Open airway, determine pulselessness, begin chest compressions, determine breathlessness, ventilate twice.

26. In general, which of the following has the greatest impact on human death rates or years of lost life in the United States?

    (A) Environment
    (B) Genetics
    (C) Lifestyle choices
    (D) Medical care

27. Getting married, beginning a new career, developing new friendships, and mastering a new physical activity most likely indicate which of the following?

    (A) Eustress
    (B) Distress
    (C) Optimal stress
    (D) Physiological stress

28. Susan ran all the way home because a large dog was chasing her. She has just slammed her front door behind her, leaving the dog barking on the sidewalk. This is an example of what phase of General Adaptation Syndrome?

    (A) Adaptive phase
    (B) Alarm phase
    (C) Exhaustion phase
    (D) Resistance phase

29. Which of the following structures is responsible for direct exchanges of oxygen and carbon dioxide in the lung?

    (A) Trachea
    (B) Alveoli
    (C) Bronchioles
    (D) Bronchi

30. The quadriceps femoris is a part of which of the following body systems?

    (A) Nervous system
    (B) Immune system
    (C) Digestive system
    (D) Muscular system

31. Aerobic exercise is best described as an activity that requires

    (A) little or no oxygen to generate energy
    (B) oxygen to generate energy
    (C) strength and speed to generate energy
    (D) flexibility to generate energy

32. Which of the following would NOT be an appropriate test to assess cardiorespiratory endurance?

   (A)   The 12-minute swim test
   (B)   The one-mile run test
   (C)   The step test
   (D)   The hand-grip test

33. The primary reason for including protein in the human diet is to provide

   (A)   material for building and repairing body tissue
   (B)   an energy reserve in the body
   (C)   vitamins and minerals for growth
   (D)   readily available energy for bodily functions

34. Eighty percent of Americans will suffer from lower-back pain in their lifetime. The primary cause of this condition is

   (A)   car accidents
   (B)   muscular imbalance of the trunk
   (C)   falls
   (D)   osteoporosis

35. The process of change illustrated in the stages of change theory (transtheoretical model) includes all of the following EXCEPT

   (A)   contemplation
   (B)   countering
   (C)   action
   (D)   termination

36. Which of the following stages of recovery described by Richard Rawson involves a period of discouragement during which relapses increase?

   (A)   Withdrawal
   (B)   Adjustment
   (C)   Resolution
   (D)   The wall

37. Which of the following statements characterizes medical quackery?

   (A)   It takes advantage of recognized laboratory procedures.
   (B)   It often uses testimonials for verification of its claims.
   (C)   It promotes consumer education.
   (D)   Its practitioners cannot legally send materials by the United States Postal Service.

38. Articles on appraising the health of school children are most likely to be found in the official publication of the

   (A)   American Public Health Association
   (B)   American Medical Association
   (C)   American School Health Association
   (D)   Society for Public Health Education

39. The definition of health given by the World Health Organization is based on the

   (A)   cause, cure, and prevention of disease
   (B)   physical, mental, and social aspects of health
   (C)   ability of humans to live in harmony with the environment
   (D)   promotion of health education throughout the world

40. In selecting a health-insurance plan, a consumer should insist that the policy comply with the Health Insurance Portability and Accountability Act of 1996 (HIPAA) and does which of the following?

   (A) Provides for a large number of beneficiaries
   (B) Terminates at a given age
   (C) Limits the insuring company's liability
   (D) Provides a guaranteed renewable contract

41. Voluntary health agencies and official (public) health agencies both play significant roles in the control of diseases in communities. How do their programs or emphases usually differ?

   (A) Voluntary agencies fight chronic diseases; public-health agencies fight communicable diseases.
   (B) Voluntary agencies work together to coordinate efforts and fight disease; public-health agencies work alone to fight disease.
   (C) Voluntary agencies usually focus on one or two related diseases; public-health agencies cover many diseases.
   (D) Voluntary agencies provide treatment and community educational activities; public-health agencies provide only treatment.

42. Which of the following federal agencies is responsible for approving the designation of new prescription drugs and additives as "generally recognized as safe" (GRAS) and/or "generally recognized as effective" (GRAE)?

   (A) Federal Trade Commission
   (B) Food and Drug Administration
   (C) United States Drug Enforcement Agency
   (D) Centers for Disease Control and Prevention

43. Current social policies and legislation prohibiting cigarette smoking in public places (offices, hospitals, airplanes, etc.) are primarily due to which two of the following factors?

   I. Increased awareness of the dangers of secondhand smoke
   II. A societal trend toward legislation of personal health-related behaviors
   III. Lobbying action by the tobacco industry to improve its image
   IV. A decrease in the social acceptability of smoking behavior

   (A) I and II
   (B) I and IV
   (C) II and III
   (D) III and IV

44. Which of the following correctly lists the path of the egg during ovulation?

(A) Uterus, fallopian tubes, ovaries, vagina
(B) Vagina, uterus, fallopian tubes, ovaries
(C) Fallopian tubes, ovaries, uterus, vagina
(D) Ovaries, fallopian tubes, uterus, vagina

45. "If I am allowed to live, I promise..."

The statement above reflects a sentiment characteristic of which of the following stages of dying, as described by Elisabeth Kübler-Ross?

(A) Denial
(B) Anger
(C) Bargaining
(D) Depression

46. Which of the following statements about the effects of activity on a young child's physical growth is most likely correct?

(A) The physique of an active child does not differ from that of an inactive child.
(B) Physical activity increases a child's bone density.
(C) Physical activity increases a child's maturation rate.
(D) Strenuous physical activity benefits the normal bone growth of a child.

RELATIVE GROWTH (MASS) OF VARIOUS BODY SYSTEMS FROM BIRTH TO AGE 20

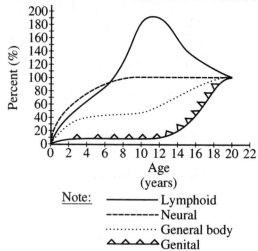

Note:
———— Lymphoid
‑‑‑‑‑‑‑ Neural
·········· General body
△△△△ Genital

47. The graph above supports which of the following statements about child development?

(A) The child's increase in strength is greatest from 10 to 12 years of age because of the development of the lymphatic system.
(B) Sex differences in height and weight in childhood can be explained by the development of the genital system.
(C) The child appears ready to learn more efficiently around 6 years of age because 95 percent of the neural system is developed.
(D) The rapid rate of growth during adolescence indicates a readiness for the development of basic motor skills.

48. The somatotype of the human body refers to the

    (A) body's size
    (B) body's shape
    (C) body's percentage of fat
    (D) relationship of body fat to size

49. In children between the ages of 5 and 7, which of the following developmental characteristics will interfere the most with their ability to engage in simple cooperative games?

    (A) Egocentricity
    (B) Lack of development of large muscles
    (C) Short attention span
    (D) Emotional immaturity

50. According to the life-span developmental approach to health education, all of the following statements are true EXCEPT:

    (A) Heredity is more influential than is environment.
    (B) Critical life events help to shape behaviors.
    (C) People can learn from the experiences of others if the experiences are similar to their own.
    (D) Development occurs during the entire life span.

51. When Susan and John are together, John lets Susan make all of the decisions. Even if he does not like her decision, John still does what Susan wants. Which of the following best characterizes John's behavior?

    (A) Assertive
    (B) Aggressive
    (C) Passive
    (D) Resistant

52. Which of the following factors is LEAST likely to contribute to an act of violence?

    (A) Having guns in the home
    (B) Witnessing a violent act
    (C) Discussing violence in school
    (D) Abusing alcohol and other drugs

53. Which of the following statements best describes how health educators view diversity?

    I.   The major dimensions of diversity are race, ethnicity, and culture.
    II. Diversity is inclusive rather than exclusive.
    III. The health status of racial and ethnic minority populations lags behind that of White Americans.

    (A) I and II only
    (B) I and III only
    (C) II and III only
    (D) I, II, and III

54. Which of the following statements is an example of an "I" message?

    (A) "I feel overburdened when I need to clean the entire house. I need your help."
    (B) "I won't listen to you because you are not listening to me."
    (C) "I am not responsible for your mistakes."
    (D) "I think you are a lazy member of this family."

55. Which of the following best describes a relationship in which a person engages with only one sexual partner during the duration of the relationship?

(A) Monogamy
(B) Open relationship
(C) Companionship
(D) Cohabitation

56. Which of the following is considered effective in preventing pregnancy and sexually transmitted infections?

(A) Norplant
(B) Diaphragm
(C) Oral contraceptives
(D) Condoms

57. Which of the following refers to a form of well-being that emphasizes the need for discovering a meaning and a purpose for life and that endows the individual with some form of ethics, values, and morals?

(A) Social wellness
(B) Spiritual wellness
(C) Mental wellness
(D) Physical wellness

58. Which of the following best describe the correct order of steps in the decision-making process?

I. Analyze internal and external influences.
II. Evaluate the decision.
III. Make a decision.
I.V Identify the decision to be made.
V. Describe alternatives and consequences.

(A) I, IV, II, III, V
(B) II, IV, III, I, V
(C) III, II, I, V, IV
(D) IV, I, V, III, II

59. Which of the following symptoms would NOT be associated with a depressive disorder?

(A) A weight gain or loss
(B) A lack of interest in pleasurable activities
(C) A focus on goals and ambitions
(D) A feeling of hopelessness and pessimism

60. A person is experiencing excessive thirst, loss of weight, continuous need to urinate, and extreme increase in appetite. Medical tests would most likely reveal higher than normal values of

(A) glucose in the blood
(B) homocysteine in the blood
(C) pancreatic fluids
(D) intestinal fluids

61. Which of the following psychosocial factors is essential for a feeling of physical vitality and the enjoyment of life?

(A) External locus of control and dependence on a social support system
(B) Knowledge of the etiology of illness and disability
(C) Attitudes and beliefs about susceptibility to and severity of disease
(D) Effective coping skills and a sense of efficacy and personal mastery

62. Which of the following is the most significant predisposing factor for cancer, cardiovascular problems, and diabetes?

(A) Substance abuse
(B) Insufficient insulin
(C) Obesity
(D) Low blood pressure

63. Which of the following conditions is correctly paired with its causative organism?

    (A) Chicken pox ··· bacteria
    (B) Athlete's foot ··· fungus
    (C) Gonorrhea ··· virus
    (D) AIDS ··· protozoan

64. "... Give us serenity to accept what cannot be changed, courage to change what should be changed, and wisdom to distinguish the one from the other."

    The statement above best exemplifies which of the following attributes of mental health?

    (A) Self-esteem
    (B) Identification
    (C) Adaptability
    (D) Compensation

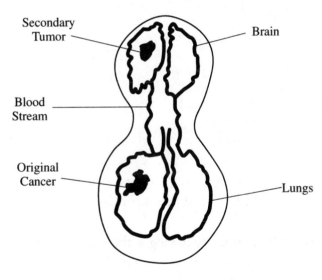

65. The diagram above suggests which of the following conditions related to cancer?

    (A) Melanoma
    (B) Metastasis
    (C) *In situ*
    (D) Sarcoma

66. Which of the following is NOT typically identified with the communicable diseases model?

    (A) Host
    (B) Agent
    (C) Environment
    (D) Risk

67. Which of the following is NOT commonly identified as a route of indirect pathogen transmission?

    (A) Air
    (B) Body fluids
    (C) Food
    (D) A vector

68. Which of the following hygienic strategies is most commonly recommended to help avoid overexposure to harmful pathogens?

    (A) Washing one's hands frequently
    (B) Washing dishes in a sanitizing dishwasher
    (C) Washing clothes using antibacterial detergents
    (D) Using an antibacterial mouthwash each day

69. Overall program goals for comprehensive school health education should include which three of the following?

    I.   Prevention of chronic disease
    II. Promotion of personal and social well-being
    III. Enhancement of decision-making skills
    IV. Increased longevity
    V.   Reduction of genetic risk factors

    (A) I, II, and III
    (B) I, III, and IV
    (C) II, IV, and V
    (D) III, IV, and V

70. Attitude scales can be important for measuring the

(A) effectiveness of an educational program
(B) academic achievement of students
(C) level of knowledge attained by individuals
(D) intellectual skills of program trainees

71. The health behaviors that should receive the highest priority for intervention in a health education program should meet which of the following pairs of criteria?

	Importance	Be Effectively Changeable
(A)	High	Changeable
(B)	High	Not changeable
(C)	Medium	Changeable
(D)	Low	Not changeable

72. Which of the following is a characteristic of norm-referenced evaluation of student academic achievement?

(A) The status of a student is compared to that of other students.
(B) The evaluation measures specific objectives of a course.
(C) The evaluation is an absolute measure with no variance.
(D) The evaluation is a relative measure with no absolute value.

73. All of the following are considered components of a unit of instruction in health education EXCEPT

(A) behavioral objectives
(B) instructional strategies
(C) Internet resources
(D) evaluation procedures

74. Which of the following is NOT a step for helping students master health skills such as decision making?

(A) Identify the steps involved in developing the skill.
(B) Model the element of the skill.
(C) Practice the skill.
(D) Test students' knowledge of the skill.

75. Which of the following characterizes an individual's ability to judge and make distinctions in the moods, intentions, and motivations of others?

(A) Spatial intelligence
(B) Natural intelligence
(C) Interpersonal intelligence
(D) Intrapersonal intelligence

Chapter 16

Right Answers and Explanations for the Practice Test,
Health Education

▶　▶　▶　▶　▶　▶　▶　▶　▶　▶　▶　▶

Now that you have answered all of the practice questions, you can check your work. Compare your answers with the correct answers in the table below.

Question Number	Correct Answer	Content Category	Question Number	Correct Answer	Content Category
1	B	Health Education as a Discipline	39	B	Community Health Advocacy
2	B	Health Education as a Discipline	40	D	Community Health Advocacy
3	B	Health Education as a Discipline	41	C	Community Health Advocacy
4	B	Health Education as a Discipline	42	B	Community Health Advocacy
5	B	Health Education as a Discipline	43	B	Community Health Advocacy
6	A	Health Education as a Discipline	44	D	Healthy Relationships
7	B	Health Education as a Discipline	45	C	Healthy Relationships
8	D	Health Education as a Discipline	46	B	Healthy Relationships
9	A	Health Education as a Discipline	47	C	Healthy Relationships
10	A	Health Education as a Discipline	48	B	Healthy Relationships
11	B	Health Education as a Discipline	49	A	Healthy Relationships
12	C	Health Education as a Discipline	50	A	Healthy Relationships
13	C	Promoting Healthy Lifestyles	51	C	Healthy Relationships
14	C	Promoting Healthy Lifestyles	52	C	Healthy Relationships
15	A	Promoting Healthy Lifestyles	53	D	Healthy Relationships
16	D	Promoting Healthy Lifestyles	54	A	Healthy Relationships
17	C	Promoting Healthy Lifestyles	55	A	Healthy Relationships
18	C	Promoting Healthy Lifestyles	56	D	Healthy Relationships
19	D	Promoting Healthy Lifestyles	57	B	Healthy Relationships
20	A	Promoting Healthy Lifestyles	58	D	Healthy Relationships
21	B	Promoting Healthy Lifestyles	59	C	Disease Prevention
22	B	Promoting Healthy Lifestyles	60	A	Disease Prevention
23	B	Promoting Healthy Lifestyles	61	D	Disease Prevention
24	C	Promoting Healthy Lifestyles	62	C	Disease Prevention
25	B	Promoting Healthy Lifestyles	63	B	Disease Prevention
26	C	Promoting Healthy Lifestyles	64	C	Disease Prevention
27	A	Promoting Healthy Lifestyles	65	B	Disease Prevention
28	B	Promoting Healthy Lifestyles	66	D	Disease Prevention
29	B	Promoting Healthy Lifestyles	67	B	Disease Prevention
30	D	Promoting Healthy Lifestyles	68	A	Disease Prevention
31	B	Promoting Healthy Lifestyles	69	A	Health Education Pedagogy
32	D	Promoting Healthy Lifestyles	70	A	Health Education Pedagogy
33	A	Promoting Healthy Lifestyles	71	A	Health Education Pedagogy
34	B	Promoting Healthy Lifestyles	72	A	Health Education Pedagogy
35	B	Promoting Healthy Lifestyles	73	C	Health Education Pedagogy
36	D	Promoting Healthy Lifestyles	74	D	Health Education Pedagogy
37	B	Community Health Advocacy	75	C	Health Education Pedagogy
38	C	Community Health Advocacy			

Explanations of Right Answers

1. Knowledge in combination with appropriate attitudes and values can impact health behaviors. The correct answer, therefore, is B.

2. The epidemiological assessment, as presented in the precede-proceed planning model, describes the primary task of determining which health problems pose the most threat to a target population. The correct answer, therefore, is B.

3. Epidemiology is defined as the study of the nature, cause, control, and determinants of disease, disability, and death in human populations. The correct answer, therefore, is B.

4. A coordinated school health program is an "organized set of policies, procedures, and activities designed to protect and promote the health and well-being of students and staff…" (Joint Committee on Health Education Terminology, 2001). The correct answer, therefore, is B.

5. The Youth Risk Behavior Surveillance System (YRBSS) provides vital information on risk behaviors among young people to target and improve health programs more effectively. The correct answer, therefore, is B.

6. The definition of mortality is death rate. Morbidity represents the rate of illness. Therefore, the correct answer is A.

7. According to the National Health Education Standards, the four characteristics of a health-literate person are being a critical thinker and problem solver, a responsible, productive citizen, a self-directed learner, and an effective communicator. The correct answer, therefore, is B.

8. According to the National Commission for Health Education Credentialing, there are seven basic competencies for entry-level health educators. In addition to answer choices A, B, and C, the other major responsibilities include planning effective health education programs; coordinating the provision of health education services; acting as a resource person in health education; and communicating health education needs, concerns, and resources. Choice D is not one of the seven. The correct answer, therefore, is D.

9. According to the National Health Education Standards, the second type of knowledge is knowledge of process and skills as applied to health and healthy living. Both types of knowledge are implied throughout the seven standards. The correct answer, therefore, is A.

10. According to the Centers for Disease Control and Prevention (CDC) reports, statistics on teenager morbidity and mortality show that the risk increases when teens use alcohol and other drugs, engage in unsafe sexual behaviors, and engage in behaviors that result in unintentional or intentional injury. The correct answer, therefore, is A.

11. Within the coordinated school health program, physical education is described as a planned program featuring sequential instruction that is aimed at promoting lifelong physical activity. It is designed to develop basic movement skills, sports skills, and physical fitness as well as to enhance emotional, mental, and social wellness. The correct answer, therefore, is B.

12. Answer choices A, B, and D are described in the preamble to the code. Choice C is not described in the code. Therefore, the correct answer is C.

13. An aerobics program should be designed to develop cardiorespiratory fitness through activities that sustain activity levels with sufficient intensity, duration, and frequency to build adequate aerobics capacity. The correct answer, therefore, is C.

14. Adolescent problem behaviors include substance abuse, delinquency, teen pregnancy, dropping out of school, and violence. The four risk factors that are associated with families and that can lead to these problem behaviors are a family history of the problem behavior; family management problems; family conflict; favorable parental attitudes and involvement in the problem behavior. The correct answer, therefore, is C.

15. Behavioral changes that occur when someone abuses alcohol will typically vary from individual to individual. In most people, alcohol will remove usual inhibitions, allowing the individuals to act in ways that may make them more interactive, more aggressive, or depressed. The correct answer, therefore, is A.

16. Of the choices given in the question, a condom is the only choice that offers some form of a barrier to direct contact with semen or vaginal fluids. Most sexually transmitted infections are spread through the exchange of blood, semen, vaginal secretions, and in some cases maternal milk. The correct answer, therefore, is D.

17. The *Dietary Guidelines for Americans* suggest that you choose a diet that is low in saturated fat and moderate in total fat. The guidelines advocate that the food pyramid be used as a guide for food choice. This supports the recommendation that carbohydrates should be the major sources of calories in your diet. The correct answer, therefore, is C.

18. To calculate the number of calories per serving that come from fat, multiply the grams of fat listed on the product label by 9. To calculate the percent of fat in the serving size, divide the previous number (calories from fat) by the calories per serving and then multiple the result by 100 to get the percent.

Calories from fat:
        6 grams of fat × 9 calories per gram = 54 calories

Percent of fat in the serving size:
        54 calories ÷ 120 calories × 100% = 45%

The correct answer, therefore, is C.

19. In order to apply proper emergency procedures the rescuer must first remove the victim from any dangerous situation. This is to protect the safety of the victim and the rescuer. The next most critical step is to attend to the stoppage of breathing, then control the bleeding. Care for the fractures is the least important step. The correct answer, therefore, is D.

20. Most research data indicate that the leading causes of death and disability are associated with lifestyle-related behaviors. If everyone eliminated smoking and other drug use, became physically active, and practiced better dietary behaviors, then many of the chronic diseases that have replaced infectious diseases as the major health concern in the twenty-first century would be eliminated. The correct answer, therefore, is A.

21. Genital herpes is caused by herpes simplex virus (HSV). HSV remains in certain nerve cells for life and can flare up, or cause symptoms, when the body's ability to maintain itself is weakened. The correct answer, therefore, is B.

22. The subject built from a resting heart rate to maintaining a target heart rate for 20 minutes. This indicates that the subject met the requirements for a vigorous cardiovascular exercise session. The correct answer, therefore, is B.

23. One pound of fat that is gained represents 3,500 calories that are taken in but not expended. In the 30 days, the individual's calorie intake exceeded his or her calorie expenditure by 10,500 calories ($350 \times 30 = 10,500$). The weight gained, in pounds, is determined by dividing the total number of excess calories by the number of calories equivalent to 1 pound of fat ($10,500 \div 3,500 = 3$.) This individual can be expected to have gained 3 pounds of fat. The correct answer, therefore, is B.

24. Depressants are drugs that depress the central nervous system. Cocaine and methamphetamine are stimulants. LSD is classified as a hallucinogen. The correct answer, therefore, is C.

25. The procedure is to first open the airway, check whether the victim is breathing, and if not, then ventilate with two breaths. Next, check the pulse, and if there is no pulse, begin chest compressions. The correct answer, therefore, is B.

26. The leading causes of premature death are related to the behaviors of smoking, inactivity, and poor dietary patterns. The correct answer, therefore, is C.

27. Stress is a part of modern life. It can be positive or negative. Positive stress, or eustress, allows health and performance to continue to improve even though the level of stress increases. At some point, however, optimal levels of stress become too much and distress occurs, which adversely affects health and performance. The correct answer, therefore, is A.

28. Hans Selye first described the internal mechanism that helps the body remain in balance and homeostasis during stress. He discussed the concept of the General Adaptation Syndrome (GAS) as having three distinct phases: alarm phase, exhaustion phase, and resistance phase. The alarm phase is when the body is exposed to a stressor and prepares itself to combat whatever is causing the upset. The correct answer, therefore, is B.

29. The air passes through the throat into the trachea or windpipe. The trachea divides into the left and right bronchi. Like a branch, each bronchus divides again and again, becoming narrower and narrower. The smallest airways end in the alveoli, small, thin air sacs that are arranged in clusters like bunches of balloons. When you breathe in by enlarging the chest cage, the alveoli expand as air rushes in to fill the vacuum. When you breathe out, the "balloons" relax and air moves out of the lungs. Tiny blood vessels surround each of the 300 million alveoli in the lungs. Oxygen moves across the walls of the air sacs and is picked up by the blood and carried to the rest of the body. Carbon dioxide or waste gas passes into the air sacs from the blood and is breathed out. The correct answer, therefore, is B.

30. The quadriceps femoris (quadriceps extensor) includes the four muscles on the front of the thigh and belongs to the muscular system. The correct answer, therefore, is D.

31. During aerobic exercise the body is using oxygen to produce the energy necessary to perform cardiorespiratory effort. The correct answer, therefore, is B.

32. The hand-grip test measures muscular strength, not cardiorespiratory endurance. The correct answer, therefore, is D.

33. Proteins are major components of nearly every cell because of their role in the development and repair of bone, muscle, skin, and blood cells. The correct answer, therefore, is A.

34. Lower-back pain may result from muscular damage, dislocation, fracture, or other problems with spinal vertebrae or discs. The correct answer, therefore, is B.

35. The stages of change include precontemplation, contemplation, preparation, action, maintenance, and termination (Prochaska, DiClemente, and Norcross, 1992). The correct answer, therefore, is B.

36. The five basic stages of recovery proposed in 1988 by Richard Rawson are 1) withdrawal, 2) honeymoon, 3) the wall, 4) adjustment, and 5) resolution. These stages continue to be applied today in various addiction settings. Withdrawal is the painful physical effects of terminating the drug use or other addictive behavior. The honeymoon is an energetic and confident time period that may be characterized by a false sense of the difficulty associated with recovery. The wall stage is a point of discouragement during which relapses increase. Adjustment is the result of working through the intense challenge of the wall. The resolution stage occurs about six months into recovery and marks a shift from learning how to recover to maintaining the necessary lifestyle. The correct answer, therefore, is D.

37. Many who make claims about the effectiveness of a product or procedure have no training or verifiable expertise in the health-related area. Many testimonials are presented by paid actors or by people who may not be telling the complete truth. The correct answer, therefore, is B.

38. The American School Health Association has a mission to "protect and improve the well-being of school children and youth by supporting comprehensive school health programs." Its main publication is the *Journal of School Health*. Although the other organizations will likely have articles in their journals about school health, this is not their primary focus. The correct answer, therefore, is C.

39. The World Health Organization defines health as "the state of complete mental, physical, and social well-being, not merely the absence of disease or infirmity." The correct answer, therefore, is B.

40. HIPAA protects health insurance coverage for workers and their families when they change or lose their jobs. HIPAA lowers workers' chances of losing existing coverage, eases their ability to switch health plans, and/or helps them buy coverage independently if they lose coverage from their employers and have no other coverage available. The correct answer, therefore, is D.

41. Voluntary health agencies were established in response to communities' perception that their needs relative to certain diseases and disorders were not being met. The primary purposes of voluntary agencies are to raise funds for research, provide educational information to both professional and public groups, and provide specific services to those affected by specific disease(s) or health condition(s). The correct answer, therefore, is C.

42. The GRAS and GRAE lists are updated and reviewed by the Food and Drug Administration. The correct answer, therefore, is B.

43. Research has confirmed the long-held belief that cigarette smoking is a health risk to non-smokers as well as to smokers. For several years, governmental advertising has attempted to reduce the number of smokers, and accompanying legislation has reduced or eliminated smoking opportunities in public places. Although once fashionable, smoking is now considered an unhealthy and unwelcome behavior among many people. The correct answer, therefore, is B.

44. The egg is formed in the ovary. Only answer choice D begins with the appropriate organ of the body. The correct answer, therefore, is D.

45. The five stages of dying introduced by Elizabeth Kübler-Ross are denial, anger, bargaining, depression, and acceptance. In the bargaining stage, the dying person may resolve to be a better person in return for an extension of life. The correct answer, therefore, is C.

46. Research shows that exercise has little effect, either positive or negative, on the growth of long bones. However, research strongly supports the idea that exercise increases bone density while inactivity is associated with bone decalcification. Studies of astronauts and bedridden patients were the primary source of these data. The correct answer, therefore, is B.

47. The actual data depicted in the graph are correctly explained by answer choice C, which is the correct answer.

48. The three somatotypes are mesomorphic (muscular), endomorphic (round and soft), and ectomorphic (tall and thin). They refer to the shape of an individual's body. The correct answer, therefore, is B.

49. Egocentric children generally view their world by assuming that others experience the world in exactly the same way they do. Therefore, working together with others in a cooperative game situation would be difficult for them. The correct answer, therefore, is A.

50. Most developmental theories acknowledge that both heredity (genetics) and the environment contribute to an individual's development, with neither having an inherent superiority over the other. The correct answer, therefore, is A.

51. Assertive people express a strong self and get what they want but not at the expense of others. Passive people are timid and shy and often feel they are being used or taken advantage of by others. Aggressive people tend to take advantage of other people and command their own agenda. The correct answer, therefore, is C.

52. Data indicate that having a gun present in the home, watching a violent act (in person or in the media), and abusing drugs are associated with violent acting out. The correct answer, therefore, is C.

53. The major dimensions of diversity are usually described as race, ethnicity, and culture. The concept of diversity in health education acknowledges that people of different racial and ethnic backgrounds may experience differences in health status and in degree of health risks because of certain beliefs and practices. Attitudes of majority groups toward minority groups may also play a role. To improve health status, programs must be inclusive and address the health needs of many different groups. The correct answer, therefore, is D.

54. "I" messages are direct, clear, and effective ways of sending information to others—messages in which a person takes responsibility for communicating his or her own beliefs, thoughts, and feelings by using statements that begin with "I" and not "you." A good practice is to begin by stating the problem with a "when you" statement. Then express how you feel with an "I feel" statement. Finally, add a statement to express your reasons for your concern such as "because." The correct answer, therefore, is A.

55. Monogamy is an exclusive sexual involvement with one partner at a time. Open relationships are based on an agreement that sexual activity can occur with other partners outside the relationship. Cohabitation is living together without being married. The correct answer, therefore, is A.

56. While all of the methods listed are used as contraceptives, only condoms serve as a barrier to transmission of infectious disease. The correct answer, therefore, is D.

57. In the study of spiritual health, most definitions include the ideas that spirituality involves the quest for an understanding of life and how one can develop a path that dictates a moral direction within one's sphere of community, society, or group. The correct answer, therefore, is B.

58. Steps in the decision-making process include identifying the decision to be made (IV), analyzing internal and external influences (I), describing alternatives and consequences (V), making a decision (III), then evaluating the decision (II). The correct order is IV, I, V, III, and II. The correct answer, therefore, is D.

59. Symptoms of depression include insomnia or oversleeping, weight gain or loss, restlessness, irritability, difficulty concentrating, physical symptoms such as headaches, decreased energy, lack of interest in sex or other pleasurable activities, a feeling of hopelessness, and pessimism. The correct answer, therefore, is C.

60. The symptoms described in the question are among those associated with diabetes. Diabetes mellitus is a condition associated with the pancreas' inability to produce sufficient insulin to help regulate blood glucose levels in cells. The correct answer, therefore, is A.

61. Practicing effective behaviors involves a belief in your abilities to perform successfully. Along with those beliefs, one needs to have acquired the skills necessary to be successful. Among these skills is the ability to recognize stressors and to cope adequately with life's daily challenges. The correct answer, therefore, is D.

62. As the second leading cause of preventable death in the United States, obesity is associated with many of the serious health problems that plague our society—the most significant of which is coronary heart disease. The correct answer, therefore, is C.

63. Chicken pox and AIDS are caused by viruses. Gonorrhea is caused by bacteria. The only correct association is the listing of athlete's foot caused by a fungus. The correct answer, therefore, is B.

64. The first step in eliminating an undesirable behavior is to recognize that there is a problem and to realize that one has the ability to change. Change is a process that involves moving progressively through certain steps, from contemplating a change to initiating a change and maintaining that change or adapting to a new lifestyle. The correct answer, therefore, is C.

65. Melanoma is a group of malignant neoplasms that usually appear on the skin. *In situ* describes a cancer that has not metastasized or invaded neighboring tissue. Sarcoma is a malignant neoplasm of the soft tissues. The diagram shows a cancer that has metastasized, or spread from the original site to create a cancer in a secondary site. The correct answer, therefore, is B.

66. The communicable diseases model is usually portrayed as a triangle that describes the interaction of the host, agent, and environment. The correct answer, therefore, is D.

67. Indirect means of pathogen transmission are air, water or food, and a vector. Transmission of disease through exchange of body fluids is a direct means of pathogen transmission. The correct answer, therefore, is B.

68. The simple practice of washing your hands is a primary method of avoiding exposure to many of the pathogens that lead to common illnesses such as colds and flu. The correct answer, therefore, is A.

69. A school health program can help prevent chronic disease, promote personal wellness, and enhance decision-making skills. However, a school health program cannot impact genetic factors or ensure a longer life for the program participants. The correct answer, therefore, is A.

70. Only answer choice A is an outcome that may be measured through the assessment of attitudes. The other choices involve assessment of intellectual or academic skills. The correct answer, therefore, is A.

71. The program should focus on the area or behaviors of highest importance that can also be effectively changed. The correct answer, therefore, is A.

72. Norm-referenced evaluation is based on a comparison of students against some standard measurement based on the performance of other students. A criterion-referenced evaluation compares students against an absolute standard measure and not against other students. The correct answer, therefore, is A.

73. Although use of the Internet would be an effective component of an instructional lesson, it is not considered a stand-alone component of a unit of instruction within health education. The correct answer, therefore, is C.

74. The National Health Education Standards identify the following five steps: introduce the skill, identify the steps involved in developing the skill, model the elements of the skill, practice the skill, and provide feedback and reinforcement. The correct answer, therefore, is D.

75. The ability to judge and make distinctions in the moods, intentions, and motivations of others describes interpersonal intelligence. The correct answer, therefore, is C.

Chapter 17

Are You Ready? Last-Minute Tips

▶ ▶ ▶ ▶ ▶ ▶ ▶ ▶ ▶ ▶ ▶ ▶

Checklist

Complete this checklist to determine whether you're ready to take the test.

❑ Do you know the testing requirements for your teaching field in the state(s) where you plan to teach?

❑ Have you followed all of the test registration procedures?

❑ Do you know the topics that will be covered in each test you plan to take?

❑ Have you reviewed any textbooks, class notes, and course readings that relate to the topics covered?

❑ Do you know how long the test will take and the number of questions it contains? Have you considered how you will pace your work?

❑ Are you familiar with the test directions and the types of questions for the test?

❑ Are you familiar with the recommended test-taking strategies and tips?

❑ Have you practiced by working through the practice test questions at a pace similar to that of an actual test?

❑ If you are repeating a Praxis Series™ Assessment, have you analyzed your previous score report to determine areas where additional study and test preparation could be useful?

The Day of the Test

You should have ended your review a day or two before the actual test date. And many clichés you may have heard about the day of the test are true. You should

- Be well rested

- Take photo identification with you

- Take a supply of well-sharpened #2 pencils (at least three)

- Eat before you take the test, and take some food or a snack to keep your energy level up

- Be prepared to stand in line to check in or to wait while other test takers are being checked in

You can't control the testing situation, but you can control yourself. Stay calm. The supervisors are well trained and make every effort to provide uniform testing conditions, but don't let it bother you if the test doesn't start exactly on time. You will have the necessary amount of time once it does start.

You can think of preparing for this test as training for an athletic event. Once you've trained, and prepared, and rested, give it everything you've got. Good luck.

Appendix A
Study Plan Sheet

► ► ► ► ► ► ► ► ► ► ►

Study Plan Sheet

See Chapter 1 for suggestions on using this Study Plan Sheet.

STUDY PLAN						
Content covered on test	How well do I know the content?	What material do I have for studying this content?	What material do I need for studying this content?	Where could I find the materials I need?	Dates planned for study of content	Dates completed

Appendix B
For More Information

▶   ▶   ▶   ▶   ▶   ▶   ▶   ▶   ▶   ▶   ▶   ▶

Educational Testing Service offers additional information to assist you in preparing for the Praxis Series™ Assessments. *Tests at a Glance* booklets and the *Registration Bulletin* are both available without charge (see below to order). You can also obtain more information from our Web site: www.ets.org/praxis/index.html.

General Inquires

Phone: 609-771-7395 (Monday-Friday, 8:00 a.m. to 8:00 p.m., Eastern time)
Fax: 609-771-7906

Extended Time

If you have a learning disability or if English is not your primary language, you can apply to be given more time to take your test. The *Registration Bulletin* tells you how you can qualify for extended time.

Disability Services

Phone: 609-771-7780
Fax: 609-771-7906
TTY (for deaf or hard-of-hearing callers): 609-771-7714

Mailing Address

Teaching and Learning Division
Educational Testing Service
P.O. Box 6051
Princeton, NJ 08541-6051

Overnight Delivery Address

Teaching and Learning Division
Educational Testing Service
Distribution Center
225 Phillips Blvd.
P.O. Box 77435
Ewing, NJ 08628-7435

DATE DUE

OCT 02 2012	
OCT 02 2012	
OCT 03 2012	
NOV 1 4 2012	
FEB 1 2 2013	

DEMCO, INC. 38-2931